Crowdfunding
INTELLIGENCE

Published by
LID Publishing Ltd
1 Mercer Street, Covent Garden,
London WC2H 9QJ

31 West 34th Street, Suite 7004,
New York, NY 10001, US

info@lidpublishing.com
www.lidpublishing.com

A member of:

www.businesspublishersroundtable.com

Printed in Great Britain by TJ International
ISBN: 978-1-907794-98-8

Cover and page design: Laura Hawkins

Crowdfunding
INTELLIGENCE

THE NO-NONSENSE GUIDE TO RAISING
INVESTMENT FUNDS ON THE INTERNET

Chris Buckingham

LONDON   MONTERREY
MADRID   SHANGHAI
MEXICO CITY   BOGOTA
NEW YORK   BUENOS AIRES
BARCELONA   SAN FRANCISCO

TO HARRIET AND MELITA

ACKNOWLEDGEMENTS:

The LID team: Martin, David, Niki and Kyomi.

Proof Perfect: Virginia Hartley who first made me realise the real value in writing something like this.

Giacomo Sardelli - just for being so brilliant

Jane Gamble for being a true friend and trusted guide.

Prof. Ashok Ranchhod at the University of Southampton for his trust, insightfulness, clarity and criticism.

Simon Whitbread for his accurate suggestions and comments.

David Brine of Hampshire Business Magazine for his trust with my monthly column.

To Annabel Arndt on Theatre Production and Dr. Loykie Lomine on Cultural and Arts Management at University of Winchester, for allowing me to 'tell & test' some of the ideas with their students.

Sally Bibb for her contribution in the creation of this book.

To Juxdit - for helping to get the word out there.

To all my Twitter followers - for helping mould this book into what we see today.

Finally, but by no means least to my family, whose support and guidance was beyond what was called for and have made me realise how very lucky I am.

CONTENTS

WHAT IS CROWDFUNDING?

It starts with a vision…

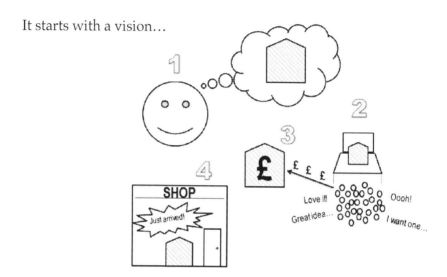

1. Imagine you have a vision you wish to create, but this vision needs funding

2. You decide to show the public your vision and ask them to help fund it

3. The public likes the idea and each person contributes a small amount of cash

4. You get to create the vision and say thanks to members of the public by giving them something back

INTRODUCTION

Crowdfunding's time has arrived. But there is a problem with the literature.

Much of the written material about crowdfunding is based on the US and tends to examine major successes that have used the crowdfunding model. This is great if you want to build the next Google or Microsoft, but if you don't, then this book is still for you. It is a little step towards redressing this imbalance by offering you, the reader, a view from the UK, within the context of the smaller success stories.

These stories have emerged when producers have managed to raise enough money to put on shows; archaeologists, through their passion and commitment, have been able to excavate sites; authors have managed to get enough people behind them to write their books; craft artisans have used the model to create their visions; and community projects have been able to add value in their local areas.

Crowdfunding represents one of the most exhilarating ways of raising funds for your project. It enables you to gain exposure in the public domain and a seal of approval for your ideas from the masses.

Crowdfunding is not a new phenomenon and has been around in different forms for a while. It developed from crowdsourcing, where people get together to solve problems. For example, there may be a need to find a new way of delivering a product to clients or to create a new design for a local skate park. The crowd helps to generate the ideas behind these initiatives. In a way, crowdfunding is an extension of crowdsourcing; only now the crowd adds money (funding) to a project. It offers solutions to project needs in all sorts of fields, from technology to zoos.

There has been a lot of talk about broken banking systems and the need for change, but change is often very slow. Maybe we are witnessing a shift as people turn away from the traditional forms of retail and commercial banking and seek a more ethical and transparent way of raising money. Peer- to-peer lending fits these criteria and organizations like Ratesetter and Zopa are at the vanguard of this field here in the UK.

All this change fits well with the contemporary concept of the maker/ DIY culture and the collaborative society, which has slowly gained traction over the past few years. Personas behind these concepts have gained near 'hero' status as saviours of our economies and structural systems. Books have emerged and become bestsellers. Talks are provided on TED.tv and other video-based sites where guru messages flirt with the viewer, convincing them that they, the experts, know best while the truth is, this is a phenomenon on your terms, in your time, on your patch and with your permission. We are all members of the crowd. We are the audience, the creators and the judges of this stuff that's getting produced.

In the 1990s, pop act Snap! had a hit with a track, featuring rapper Turbo B, called *I've Got the Power*. If this were to be released today, the title might be 'We've got the power' - simply because we have.
This book will also look at the dark side of crowdfunding.

This is the negative aspect of crowdfunding, but not a side that needs to be feared. Raising your required funding is – as we shall see – only one aspect of this very social way of raising awareness about your vision.

It is the planning stages on which we largely concentrate in this book; we aim to provide you with a guide that will help you tap into the vast potential of crowdfunding. As authors, we are in a position to offer this advice because we have been observing and helping stakeholders in this phenomenon for a number of years.

What we are really attempting to do here is to add value for you through our research and development of models for success. To this end, we have developed the Crowdfunding Planning Page, a useful and practical resource that will aid your campaign before, during and after the launch of your crowdfunding challenge.

Make no mistake, it is a challenge. Crowdfunding, like most things in life, looks easy when you look at successful examples, retrospectively. Isn't it obvious they were always going to succeed? Well, not to the project team before it reached its targets. Crowdfunding needs careful planning, sweat, tears and passion for success to be achieved. So before you march straight in, please read this book, reflect on the contents and plan, plan, plan.

You are about to start one of the most amazing journeys, so let's ensure you have everything you might need along the way.

We begin with some definitions:

TABLE I: USEFUL DEFINITIONS

TERM	DEFINITION
APPLICANT	Person or team seeking value from the crowd
CAMPAIGN	The temporary pitch made to the crowd
FUNDER	The person or team backing the campaign
MODEL	One of five crowdfunding options with the acronym DREIM*
PLATFORM	The online place from where the pitch is presented to the crowd

*DREIM = Donation, Reward, Equity, Interest (debt) and Mixed.

SECTION 1:
FOUNDATIONS

CONTENTS

1.1

CROWDSOURCING

People acting together to achieve a pre-defined goal is nothing new. It has probably been happening for millennia. What is new, is the means of communicating and arranging for your needs to be met. Instead of relying on geographical neighbours and family we can now achieve similar results with people many thousands of miles away from us. That's a really powerful concept and one that defines our age.

Before we begin, it might be useful for us to take stock and define what we mean by crowdsourcing and funding. A brilliant definition of these was written by Brian Rubinton in an academic paper he published in 2011.[2] He stated that crowdsourcing was:

"...the process of one party progressing towards a goal by requesting and receiving small contributions from many parties in exchange for a form of value to those parties."

He then wrote that crowdfunding was:

"...the process of one party financing a project by requesting and receiving small contributions from many parties in exchange for a form of value to those parties."

The term crowdsourcing was first used in 2006 by American, Chris Anderson.[3] He famously wrote an article for *Wired* magazine entitled *The Rise of Crowdsourcing*. For the first time, the masses in the networked social worlds we inhabit were seen as entrepreneurial entities with the ability to sustain their activities. For Anderson, this started in 2004 with a medical institution seeking photos of ill people to use in their promotional materials. What this institution found was that, rather than paying for photographer to take the photos they required, they could buy a whole range of suitable photos from a website with hundreds of cheap images.

These images were cheap because they were taken and supplied by amateurs in their spare time. But what made this group special was the fact they were also making a bit of money on the side by selling their photography. Some were superb quality. Many of the contributors had ordinary day jobs and spent all their free time on their hobby.

This story is important because it highlights the very essence of the rise of the pro-am class. Products that were, at one time, the exclusive tools of the professional class (in this case, expensive cameras) were now becoming cheap enough for anyone to buy. What's more, amateur photographers could learn to use this equipment online for free. Through the online communities within which they interacted. they were spreading their know-how, tips, 'dos and don'ts', all for free. What these people gained in return was a form of social capital, a kind of prestige for being the best there was at that particular aspect of photography or even the business models they used to distribute and sell their work.

The aformentioned example presents an obvious problem for the professional photographer; their business model is no about longer competing with other professional photographers who market themselves as having specialist knowledge and expensive equipment. There has been an explosion in the number of amateur photographers selling sophisticated images at just a few pounds each.

Those wanting images now have a huge selection from which to choose, at low prices. Software means that these images can also be manipulated to create effects that are superior to the original image. In short, amateurs can learn to use free software, like GIMP (GNU Image Manipulation Program), to add value to their photographs. They can share their work via sites dedicated to selling their creations, or offer them for free, all with feedback and 'feedforward' from their peers. If they are lucky, the pictures may even go viral.

Further Up Yonder, a short video compiled from images from the international space station, edited together by Giacomo Sardelli, a young man from the north of Italy, did just that. In late 2012, he stitched together speeded-up time-lapse images of planet Earth with poignant voice-overs from astronauts, and posted it to Vimeo. Within a week, the video had received more than 100,000 views, he had been featured in the *Guardian* newspaper in the UK and interviewed for the BBC's *Newsround* programme. Sardelli had the vision, NASA had the images, DigitalR3public created the soundtrack *Synthetic Truth*. These were combined by Sardelli to create a wonderful piece of cinema that the world was free to share, watch and wonder at.[4]

These are powerful tools created, not by huge corporations in their offices in major cities, but by individuals who have a passion for a hobby, whether this is software development or photography. This can all be done outside the boundaries and restrictions of traditional copyright by employing the Creative Commons licence. This allows creators to share their work with others who can build on the original, creating something fresh as a result.

But *Further Up Yonder* is not just about crowdsourcing materials for a project. This is about the amateur doing it for the sake of doing it. Had NASA asked for such a video to be created, we would indeed be talking about a brilliant creation that fulfilled another function, beyond the purpose for which *Further Up Yonder* was actually created (art).

Developing an artistic creation is not necessarily the same thing as creating for crowdsourcing. Remember Brian Rubinton's words at the opening of this section. Sardelli's story is not about "the process of one party progressing towards a goal by requesting and receiving small contributions from many parties in exchange for a form of value to those parties", it is about one party (Sardelli) creating value for many parties (the crowd) because he could. He had the will to do it, the technology and the vision. He was also able, cognitively, to put all this together.

Sardelli may go on to become a top film producer, he obviously has talent, and may even be asked by NASA to compile another movie on its behalf. But again, a distinction must be made with the concept of crowdsourcing. Sardelli may be asked, not the crowd. If NASA asked the crowd – it would be sourcing that value it sought from the crowd; NASA would be crowdsourcing.

While modern politicians like to claim they have all the answers, experts certainly do not. They may be too close to the question they are asking to be in a position to answer it. By opening the question up to the crowd they can employ many, many different people from an extremely diverse range of backgrounds. This is the great strength of crowdsourcing, it allows for input on issues from those external to the culture of the field from within which the question has emerged. In other words, outsiders may be able to see the problem with fresh eyes and not be blinded by the constraints of being an expert 'in' the subject area.

We will always need experts. Crowdsourcing means the expert could be someone with a passion for the subject but not necessarily someone from within the field or sector. It could be anyone with a sufficiently deep understanding of the topic or issue, the drive to engage and the will to apply that knowledge.

Crowdsourcing is the proud parent of crowdfunding and the latter has grown rapidly in terms of media coverage and utility to its stakeholders. There are criticisms of crowdfunding and one of the more important ones has been concerned with the 'expert' voice. Generally, this argument is that the previous system of raising finance through venture capitalists, business angels or business bankers, meant more advice and input from experts on the development of new entrepreneurial projects.

Their input was greater than just the money they would give or lend to the business. They might add value through their contacts, knowledge of systems, networks and infrastructure that could be at the disposal of the entrepreneur once the expert was on board.

Crowdfunding changes this situation, especially for the creative industries, by allowing the project manager (entrepreneur) to gain the funds needed to realize the project without having to convince a venture capitalist, business angel or bank employee of its worth. More than this, the project manager can now do this on their *own* terms. This is because people are now more in control than ever before.

This is not suggesting an easier route to finance can be found in crowdfunding, applicants still have to convince the crowd to help them, via well thought-out, detailed, plans and pitches. But amateurs and professionals alike can help in this emergent method.

Amateurs are able to pass on helpful tips to other amateurs using social media tools. This advice could be about price, usage or even where to find face-to-face help. Social media facilitates this exchange and makes these interactions, for whatever purpose, possible.

For the creative industries, this is a massive change in their favour. A report by Professor Stuart Fraser, published in 2011[5] , found that the creative industries were often misunderstood by financial institutions. Finance was more difficult for this sector than for other comparable sectors. There were a number of reasons cited, but one stood out as prominent, and it applies to crowdfunding just as much as it does to traditional means of raising finance for a project: it is 'moral hazard'.

Moral hazard is the use of the capital raised for purposes other than those stated. For example, imagine I am a visual artist working with glass and decide to buy a new furnace to heat my glass. I ask the people with the money to provide £2,000 and they decide to lend me the money. I receive £2,000 and then, instead of using it to buy the furnace, I spend that money on paying my bills. This is an example of moral hazard. I have used the cash for purposes other than those stated when I initially requested the money.

For the lenders in the old system, this was a problem; they had lent me £2,000 for the purchase of an asset that had monetary value - it was a physical asset with monetary value. If things had gone wrong and I had gone bankrupt, the investors would have lost some money but they might have also been able to sell the furnace and recoup a little of the lost money. In the moral hazard scenario, I have used the money for another purpose; once the bills are paid the money has gone - there is no asset for the people who are owed the money to sell on.

This example is very simplistic and moral hazard has always been a real risk factor when lending institutions are approached by anyone, let alone the creative industries. It is also very difficult to predict the winning formula for a piece of theatre or art. Added to this is the challenge of understanding what will be the next *Mousetrap*[6] or who will be the next Rothko.[7] It is almost impossible to predict with any certainty.

Experts who lend money like certainty, or at least the mirage of certainty, and this has been the other side of the problem for the creative industries: the risks are deemed to be too high for traditional lenders. However, a new star has now taken centre stage for this and many more sectors - that new star is crowdfunding.

Crowdfunding is not just useful for the creative industries - it is a sound funding route for many sectors. There are still dangers with it and crowdfunding is not an easy route to getting your project funded, there are many factors that need considering before you enter the public domain.

Crowdfunding has the potential to effect massive change in the way we do things. It means the gatekeepers who previously decided whether or not a potential project received funding are no longer as relevant. Decisions about the value of a theatrical show or of the work of a sculptor can now be decided by the public. Even manufactured goods can be 'tested' before production begins. Crowdfund a possible product or piece of art and see how the public reacts; if people like it, it gains the funding needed and if they don't, it doesn't. Simple.

For products or services, this also allows the producer the opportunity of gauging the size of a potential market. They may be able to presell products or tickets before committing too many resources. This is really valuable information and an area of crowdfunding we shall explore in much more detail later in the book.

1.2

CROWDFUNDING PATHS AND MODELS

First we need to establish that crowdfunding a *project* is an *entrepreneurial* activity that, if successful in raising funds, will mean an opportunity being realized. Therefore, before we detail the models available in crowdfunding, let's take a moment to define exactly what we mean. To define an entrepreneurial opportunity we shall turn to the words of brilliant British author, David Rae:

"The opportunity may be a situation which already exists, or one which we create and which would not otherwise have occurred. An opportunity may be one which we can actually recognize now, or one which will arise in the future. Types of opportunity may include, for example:

- a 'gap in the market' for a product or service
- a mismatch between supply and demand
- a future possibility which can be recognized or created

- a problem that can be solved, for example, by applying a solution to a need
- a more effective or efficient business process, system or model
- a new or existing technology or approach which has not yet been applied
- the transfer of something that works in one situation to another, such as a product, process or business concept
- a commodity or experience people would desire or find useful if they knew about it." [8]

It is important to distinguish between peer-to-peer (p2p) personal finance and p2p project finance as these are the two paths available in crowdfunding (see figure 1.2.1).

FIGURE 1.2.1: CROWDFUNDING PATHS

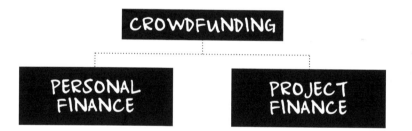

Personal finance is the borrowing and lending of money for personal purposes. This could be for a car, boat or extension to a home. There can be any number of reasons why people borrow money in this category, but the use of the money borrowed is for something *personal*.

Project finance, on the other hand, will refer here to the use of money borrowed for the purposes of an *entrepreneurial opportunity*. 'Project' can mean many things, and indeed the extension of a house or the purchase of a boat can be classed as a project, but for the purposes of this book, a project will be defined as an entrepreneurial opportunity, in its broadest sense. This is an important definition because an entrepreneurial opportunity, in this sense, may not be a sustainable opportunity. It may be ephemeral in nature.

In other words, the opportunity may not be one that will last long term, in the traditional business model sense. It may be a simple model that is project-based.

The project manager in this circumstance opens the project, completes the task requested and then closes the project before moving on to the next one. This model is common in the creative industries. It is ephemeral because the project may only exist for a short space of time.

Think about a one-off theatre production; let us call it *'The Play'*. It is planned, executed and then shelved until a possible future performance can be arranged. But the management, the technical team and the actors will probably move on to other productions where they will be working alongside a completely new team.

So although they continue to function with different shows and possibly in different geographical locations, *'The Play'* becomes ephemeral - only existing for a fleeting moment.

This unique model can often be seen in the creative industries where projects are available or functioning for a temporary (and possibly specific) time and place. This is counter to the sustainable development of a traditional entrepreneurial venture where one of the criteria for the opportunity is that it is able to sustain itself in economic terms.

So, there must be an income of some sort to enable the enterprise to continue. Even if it is a social enterprise, there still needs to be some form of income to enable the enterprise to function on its own without continually applying for funding from awards or grants.

There may well be instances where personal lending has been used for the purposes of funding an entrepreneurial project. Parallels exist here with the entrepreneur and/or artist using their credit card or personal overdraft facility in order to finance their vision.

Some literature will class crowdfunding as both p2p personal finance and p2p project finance, and, actually, this is correct as both are a form of crowdfunding. However the main focus of this book will be *project finance*.

Before getting into that, we will begin with a description of the available paths within crowdfunding and then outline the various models. We will deal first with the personal finance path and then move to the more diverse project finance path.

This is important because it sets the scene for the novice in crowdfunding and helps our understanding of the various applications of the models. Crowdfunding is nothing new; what is new is the ability to connect individuals separated by huge distances to help fund a project.

Each path has its own set of models that sit under the headline path as demonstrated in figure 1.2.2, (p30) which clearly shows the paths available in the crowdfunding milieu.

FIGURE1.2.2: CROWDFUNDING PATHS WITH MODELS

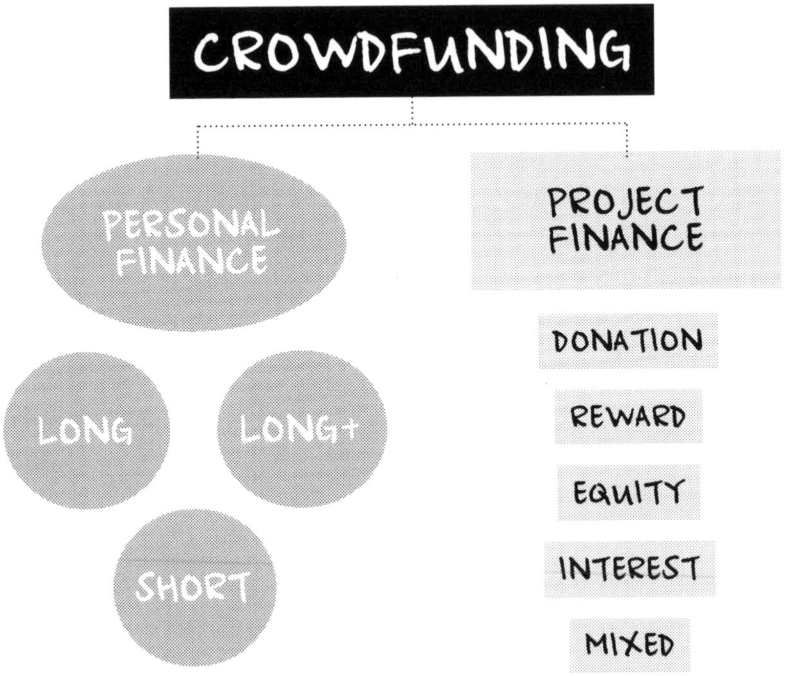

From figure 1.2.2, we can see there are two distinct paths (personal finance and project finance) with equally distinct *models* in each path.

PERSONAL FINANCE: LONG VERSUS SHORT

As a concept, personal finance crowdfunding is much more straightforward than its sister model, project finance crowdfunding. Personal finance crowdfunding is divided into three camps: long, long+ and short lending. The amounts borrowed can be for rates comparable with the market generally unless you are planning to use pay-day lending (which is short-term lending).

Zopa was the first platform to offer p2p personal finance and was established in the UK in 2005. In 2010, Ratesetter joined the market. Ratesetter and Zopa are in the long-term lending personal finance market.

At the time of writing, there are two players in the short-term lending market: Piggy Bank – a trading name of DJS (UK) Limited - incorporated with Companies House in 2012 – and The Lending Well (incorporated with Companies House in 2011). Both were closed for a time through 2013/2014 and, at the time of writing, Piggy Bank was lending money but did not appear to be accepting new lenders from the crowd. The Lending Well remained closed for business. Whether this is because of legislation, lack of demand or some other circumstance is not clear.

What is clear is that crowdfunding is a very exciting arena to be watching right now as new models and applications of the concept emerge. One such recent development has been the emergence of a platform called eMoneyUnion (incorporated with Companies House in 2012).

Before we go any further, let's summarize these models in figure 1.2.3:

FIGURE 1.2.3: SHORT VERSUS LONG MARKETS

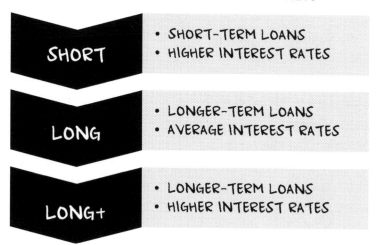

SHORT
- SHORT-TERM LOANS
- HIGHER INTEREST RATES

LONG
- LONGER-TERM LOANS
- AVERAGE INTEREST RATES

LONG+
- LONGER-TERM LOANS
- HIGHER INTEREST RATES

Long tends to be for more standard market rates and allows loans to be repaid over a longer period of time. In contrast, short (sometimes referred to as 'pay-day lending' or 'vulture lending') tends to be for shorter periods of time and interest is charged above the standard market rates. This is because these loans are perceived as higher risk and are, by their nature, for shorter periods of time.

It should, however, be noted that eMoneyUnion will lend money for up to a five-year period, but at higher rates of interest. This is justified as the individuals borrowing the money have very poor credit ratings and may even need the backing of a higher credit-rated individual as a guarantor for the loan. This is a newer application of crowdfunding and it sits below the short and long models as it offers higher-risk borrowers the opportunity to borrow from the crowdfunding market, at interest rates that reflect the risks.

Table 1.2.1 contrasts these market players in the personal finance sector and it becomes quite clear that Ratesetter has much more flexibility for the user in terms of the loan's time-span. Ratesetter offers four options to users, whereas Zopa offers just two. A question both organizations are no doubt asking is "what value does this bring the users?" Are users (both borrowers and lenders) attracted by more dynamic lending periods or do they prefer more straightforward choices? Interestingly, Zopa has changed its model in recent years, perhaps in response to market demands.

Essentially, these are strategic questions for the organizations and their business models. All business models in this sector are multi-sided in that they need the lenders to lend and the borrowers to borrow for the platform and the market generally to be sustainable. If they were to lose one or the other side of the business the market would collapse.

TABLE 1.2.1: COMPARATIVE MATRIX

(ACCESSED *17/12/12, †28/11/13 & ∞04/02/14)

PLATFORM	TERM	BORROW ( )
RATESETTER	MONTHS: 1, 12, 36, 48/60	1000 – 25000*
ZOPA	MONTHS: 36 OR UP TO 60	1000 – 20000
EMONEYUNION	MONTHS: 12 TO 60	1000 – 10000∞
PIGGY BANK	DAYS: 7 – 42 (1-HOUR LOANS ALSO POSSIBLE)	50 – 500**
THE LENDING WELL	DAYS: 10 – 31	100 – 750*

**Upper level increases to 1,000 for established borrowers

What makes these models unique is that the platforms are not actually lending any money.

They are merely acting as a meeting place for the lender and the borrower and charging a fee for fixing up the 'date' between the two. They comply with the Financial Conduct Authority rules as well as having their own code of conduct provided by the peer2peer Finance Association (launched in August 2011). This was established by Ratesetter and Zopa in the personal finance model, and funding circle in the project finance model, to set out clear rules of conduct and quality standards for the peer-to-peer *debt raising* crowdfunding industry.

It is fair to say that both Ratesetter and Zopa are similar in their business models. With the recent turmoil and depression that was felt throughout much of the economy between 2008 and 2014, this may offer some comfort to investors. These sites do not offer amazing returns, but they are relatively stable and any bad debt will be factored in to the returns they feature for your investment; in other words the platforms are trying to be as transparent as they dare, while not trying to put off would be investors.

Nothing is risk-free in investing. But at least, here, your money helps ordinary people while making a small return for you. Most people seem to agree that this is a preferable system to the impersonal corporations that were the only option in the past.

UNIQUE FEATURES

Ratesetter allows lenders and their borrowers to agree rates of interest. This works well as the lender wants to lend at a reasonable rate and get their capital returned with interest, while the borrower wants to borrow at an acceptable rate.

If borrowers try to charge higher interest than the market average, their offers will take much longer to be accepted and, in extreme cases, may not be loaned at all. This is because the borrower is free to choose the rates at which they borrow. So, by default, most will choose a rate that is considered reasonable or even 'cheap' when compared with the market generally. For lenders, Ratesetter offers a calculator that will predict how fast money will be loaned and the expected returns (including default rates). They also inform the lender if the rates are too high which acts as a means of policing the rates on offer and ensures lenders are aware of the current levels in order to maximize their lending capacity.

In effect, what Ratesetter is doing is holding the rates in equilibrium. Lenders want their monies loaned and returns paid efficiently, while borrowers want to be able to borrow at fair rates. This system ensures transparency is offered to all users of the platform. Rates are clear for all markets in all loan periods and the expected (average) default rate for the lender is also clearly set out.

Any loss due to defaults in the personal finance model is not tax deductible. A lender cannot write-off the loss against their taxable income from transactions in the personal finance path. This is different in the project finance path where the UK government has introduced schemes allowing losses to be offset against tax payment. On top of this, profits from certain types of investments are not taxed. There are two schemes called the Enterprise Investment Scheme (EIS)[13] or the Start-up Enterprise Investment Scheme (SEIS)[14.]

The platforms in the long and long+ markets have received a substantial amount of criticism for charging much higher rates than the market average. A counter-argument is that the lender is taking a bigger gamble by lending to individuals with high risk profiles. To attract lenders, the rates must be striking.

Recently, an argument has been put forward from within the industry that a form of EIS or SEIS would help this sector by attracting more lenders. Rates could thus be negotiated by the crowd and losses made more acceptable because of the favourable tax position for the lender. This is not the place to detail these arguments, but it is important the reader is aware of the criticisms often levelled at short and long+ models of lending.

Each of the highlighted companies can be mapped using the same template as Figure 1.2.3 (p31). Only here we can outline which company fits which model:

FIGURE 1.2.4: COMPANIES AND THEIR MARKET MODELS

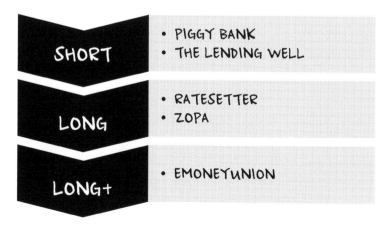

SHORT
- PIGGY BANK
- THE LENDING WELL

LONG
- RATESETTER
- ZOPA

LONG+
- EMONEYUNION

Now we have set the scene, we move on below to project finance – which is the main focus.

PROJECT FINANCE

There are four different models for crowdfunding in the project finance path. Each one differs substantially and each offers value to different business models. Using the DREIM acronym (Donation, Reward, Equity, Interest (debt) or Mixed - see figure 1.2.5) each model will be outlined below (these will be given more depth in section 2.7).

FIGURE 1.2.5: CROWDFUNDING PROJECT FINANCE MODEL.

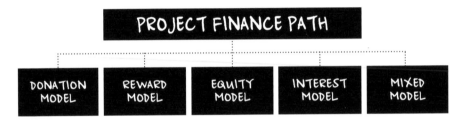

Project finance is the main focus of this book – the entrepreneurial application of the five models above to crowdfunding. David Rae provided a brilliant insight at the beginning of this book with a clear definition of what exactly an entrepreneurial opportunity is. But here we need to develop this a little further as we add layers to the complexity of the terms. Again using David Rae, let's define exactly what we mean by these terms:

- Enterprise
- Entrepreneur
- Entrepreneurship

Enterprise: if people display enterprise, it means they are using the skills, knowledge and personal attributes needed to apply creative ideas and innovations to practical solutions. These include initiative, independence, creativity, problem solving, identifying and working on opportunities, leadership, and acting resourcefully to effect change. The term 'enterprise' is also used to describe a small or new business venture.

Entrepreneur: this is the person who acts in an enterprising way, and who identifies or creates and acts on an opportunity, for example by starting a new business venture.

Entrepreneurship: this is the subject of enterprise and entrepreneurs, encompassing both the practical and academic knowledge, skills and techniques used in being an entrepreneur.
(David Rae, 2007: 3)

All three of these definitions will be used in the following pages as they apply directly to crowdfunding, and especially to the activity engaged in by the management behind the campaigns. By setting out the definitions now, we avoid confusion later. This is also an important part of managing a campaign; clear communication, as we shall see, is an essential part of the management process.

DONATION

This model is often associated with community projects and social enterprises as there is no financial return for the funder(s) who give their money. In this model, giving is a philanthropic act.

Value equates to some benefit from the project for others and this is often the motivating factor for people to give in the first place. It is possible to combine crowdfunding and crowdsourcing in this model for the purposes of generating even greater value for the project's stakeholders. Not only do donors get to do some good with their money, but they get to be involved with the project at some deeper level.

Examples include a church that needs some building work, a dance charity that requires new equipment or a local skate park in need of repair.

Often, these are local concerns that have direct benefit for the community they serve, but equally, they may be large-scale projects involving humanitarian aid for a natural disaster in a geographically-remote area of the world.

A great example of this type of platform is Deki.org.uk.[15] This organization provides micro loans to entrepreneurs in developing nations. These loans tend to be for amounts of money that are fairly insignificant to people in the UK but can have a very big impact on entrepreneurs in developing nations. The money is then paid back over a set period of time with no interest. Think of it as a loan without the interest.

For the most part, people use this service (and the US equivalent, Kiva.org[16]) as they get a 'warm glow' from doing some good and helping those in need. This is normally for the base of the pyramid, but interestingly, Kiva in the US has begun to offer this service to US citizens.

TASK 1: DONATION MODEL

LIST WHAT YOU SEE AS THE PROS AND CONS OF A DONATION MODEL FOR YOUR CAMPAIGN.

REWARD

Reward is by far the most common model of crowdfunding (especially in the creative sector). A reward can be anything that adds value for the funder of the project. It could be a signed CD or book, a personal appearance or performance, a mention in the credits or any number of other forms of value.

This is where scarcity can be a wonderful advantage in gaining more attention from the crowd. It often follows that the demand for a reward can be higher for things that are, or at least perceived to be, unique, desired and scarce (see 1.5 below).

Rewards tend to be tiered, with higher amounts of funding input gaining more significant, or more unusual, rewards. An example of a fictitious music group is given below where the reward structure is relative to the amounts of money pledged in the campaign.

So the greater the amount pledged - the greater the reward's perceived value.

TABLE 1.2.2: FICTITIOUS REWARD STRUCTURE FOR A BAND

REWARDS

GIVE £1 AND GET
For this tiny donation your name will be added to the electronic wall of fame.

GIVE £5 AND GET
As well as a mention on the wall we will give you a badge posted directly to your home, as well as that fuzzy feeling of supporting local arts. Hurray!

GIVE £10 AND GET
A silver membership card entitling you to 10% off admission FOR LIFE to every gig by the band. Oh, and of course, you will also get a super-cool badge and a mention in the credits! (295 of 300 left)

GIVE £20 AND GET
Gold membership card entitling you to 20% off admission FOR LIFE to every gig by the band as well as a T-Shirt, badge and mention in the credits. (293 of 300 left)

GIVE £100 AND GET
Supernova membership card entitling you to 20% off admission FOR LIFE, a T-Shirt and badge, mention in the credits and a shout-out live on stage in our 2014 gig. (18 of 20 left)

Note that in each of the categories, the band has listed the number of rewards remaining in the last three categories where the economic value is increasing. This is very common on most platforms and may act as an incentive for the funder as they can see how many are remaining. But could this also have the opposite effect? Could people see how many have been 'purchased' and make a decision based on this signal from others?

There is evidence in the personal finance path that this is the case, but, as yet, no empirical evidence has emerged about the effects of this in other sectors of the crowdfunding milieu, such as the reward model.

One last point to make in this section about rewards is the concept of 'stretch goals' that often appear once a campaign has hit its target. These are there to encourage the crowd to take the campaign even further by offering a higher level of reward.

For example, imagine the campaign has reached its funding goal of £1,000. But you still have 20 days of the campaign to run. Stretch goals can now be introduced to try and take the campaign to an even higher funding level. So, in this example, the applicants might want to set the stretch goal at £2,000 and offer two additional rewards to encourage the crowd to help them reach this new target.

Standard procedure with this is that even if the stretch goals are not reached, the original funding level has been reached and therefore the campaign will receive the original investment from the crowd. But it is always worth checking this with the platform with which you are dealing to ensure you are not snatching defeat from the jaws of victory. Stretch goals will be given more attention in section 3.3 (p187).

Rewards can also be offered in the equity and interest models of crowdfunding (although they are less common in the interest model).

But this works slightly different to the straight reward model in that these rewards (or gifts) are offered as an 'extra' rather than being the main focus.

In these two models (equity and interest) the reward acts as a little sweetener to incentivize the crowd to give its consent. It acts as a little something extra to say thanks for the support.

Rewards in this instance are usually something small, related to the campaign. For example, a recruitment specialist might offer a free CV health check while a clothing company might offer a free bag in which to carry clothes when travelling. These little extras come at a cost that should be covered by the raise. In other words, their cost should be funded by a small percent of the overall crowdfunding raise.

TASK 2: REWARD MODEL

THINK ABOUT OR DISCUSS THE REWARDS - WHICH DO YOU THINK ARE MORE EFFECTIVE? WHY? HOW COULD YOU TEST THESE REWARDS BEFORE GOING LIVE?

REWRITE THE ABOVE REWARDS USING YOUR OWN WORDS (ESPECIALLY THE ACTIVE VERB GIVE).

DOES THE WORDING SOUND BETTER WITH THE PASSIVE OR ACTIVE FORM?

EQUITY

This model is perhaps the most complicated (followed closely by the interest model - see p45). It is advisable to gain legal advice before you commit to offering equity in your project, although it is very common for the platforms to offer this service. There are several reasons for this: it helps them with their compliance with the FCA's regulations[10]; it can also be a part of their trade body membership; and lastly, it's in their interest to offer protection for the funder. If the funder feels more secure – they are probably more likely to engage with the campaign.

Equity basically means giving away a percentage of your project for funding.

AN EXAMPLE:

You need £500 for project 'XYZ'.

Project XYZ is valued at £1,500, so you offer 33% of the project.

So the crowd takes ownership of 33% of the organization. This is divided among the crowd members depending on the amount they actually put in to the project.

For example, Ian has invested £100 and Tasha has invested £500. Tasha now gets a slightly larger share of the 33% than Ian. However, there is also a lot of debate about how these shares will be treated in any future deals. This is because not all shares are equal, some have better terms than others. If the project wants to expand or scale-up its operations at a later date, getting a venture capitalist or other financial institution on-board could prove difficult if the original offer to the crowd is set so that it has a good percentage of the organization.

This is a very simplistic explanation, but it gives you an idea of how it works at the most basic level. Both Ian and Tasha are probably expecting a return on their investment. This can be in the form of dividends paid to them by the organization and/or selling their share once the organization has grown to a point where it is starting to make money. You can see how complicated it could become. It may also mean that future growth plans of the project are restricted because of decisions made now in the very early stages.

Another problem could manifest itself if Tasha and Ian sell their shares to another investor. It raises some important issues about how you will work with that other investor and what type of share they are dealing. A new investor might be much more demanding than Ian and Tasha or perhaps more ambitious for the project than you had intended. They may want to expand quickly and try to push you in directions that are not compatible with your own values.

Problems can arise in all kinds of ways in this model, but it can also be the best way for a fledgling project to gain traction and break into a market. It may be that Tasha is very well-connected and can open many more doors for you and the project. Maybe she will be the driving force you need to get the project established.

It is very important that you understand the investor and that the investor understands the project. In the 2011 report by Dr Stuart Fraser, obtaining finance from traditional lenders like banks was found to be more difficult for the creative sector when compared to other similar (in terms of risk profile) industries. His report also highlighted a number of instances where finance had, in principle, been agreed between the bank and the creative enterprise, only to be rejected later by the owners of the creative enterprise.

This strange situation was thought to be due, in part, to the terms offered by the lending institution. These terms sometimes meant that control and ownership of the enterprise would be shared. Generally, for the creative industries, this was not an option they favoured, and they preferred slower organic growth while maintaining control over the project.

A second element to this rejection by the creative enterprise of the finance on offer concerned security. Dr Fraser found evidence that the lending institution would, as a rule, seek higher security against their lending than they might with comparable (in terms of risk) industries.

This latter point was attributed to misunderstandings on the part of the lending institution concerning the business model and degree of risk to which they were being exposed to by undertaking the loan.

In fact, Dr Fraser found this misunderstanding was two-way, with institutions failing to understand the creative sector fully and the creative sector failing to understand the limitations and parameters of the lending institution.

Given this, perhaps it is not surprising that equity in the crowdfunding model is not the most popular form of crowdfunding for the creative industries. Equity means a degree of loss in terms of control over the project. When creatives are well known for having a clear vision of what they wish to create and the direction in which they wish the project to go, it becomes more understandable why this model is less popular in this sector.

There are three main sections on any platform's web page to look for help when considering this model, they are:

- How it works
- Frequently asked questions (FAQs)
- Terms and conditions

If you still have unanswered questions, contact the platform's customer help or support team. These teams are there to assist you and answer any questions and are, generally speaking, first class in their responses. In our experience, they are also very good at finding answers to some really tricky questions.

TASK 3: EQUITY MODEL

CHOOSE TWO PLATFORMS AND MAKE SOME NOTES ABOUT THE PROTECTION THEY OFFER INVESTORS.

WHAT DIFFERENCES HAVE YOU NOTICED IN THESE DOCUMENTS?

INTEREST

Like traditional banks where loans are made and then paid back over time with a bit extra, we see the same in this model of crowdfunding.

People invest with the expectation that the original monetary input (their capital) will be repaid in due course (the term of the agreement) plus a little extra (interest). These loans can be at slightly higher interest rates than other alternative sources of finance.

There may also be issues if the organization is seeking to obtain grants and/or awards as well as raising debt. Some funding organizations do not view debt as a positive attribute. Debt being raised through a relatively new method (such as crowdfunding) can add to these perceptions. If your organization intends to go for grants or awards, it might be better to obtain these first as debt could be a barrier to accessing these pots of money.

If you loan a friend a small amount of money, you are fairly sure that friend will pay it back, but in the interest crowdfunding model, money is being loaned to a mostly unknown entity that may have hidden problems or issues. For this reason, the ability of the crowd to ask questions and get responses from campaign management are vital.

Most platforms in this model will want two years' trading accounts and for the company to be profitable before you can apply. This acts as a check on the applicants and also ensures that the organization is a sound one – even if they get a low risk rating (most platforms are explicit about the risks involved). These checks also help prevent fraudsters from trying to get loans from the crowd.

Platforms operating this model carry out credit checks before loans are agreed. This means there is a very strong chance that fraudsters will be spotted before they engage the crowd. Of course, defaults can and do happen. But they are rarer than people might imagine.

Usually, if a default does occur, there are securities that were assigned to the loan by the applicant when they made their initial request to campaign. So the risks, although not eliminated entirely, are pretty transparent and the organizations campaigning in this model are also encouraged to respond to questions from the crowd, some members of which can add much depth to the knowledge the crowd has about the organization and its activities.

TASK 4: INTEREST MODEL

LOOK AT SOME LOAN REQUESTS (YOU WILL NEED TO REGISTER AS A LENDER) ON AT LEAST THREE PLATFORMS.

TRY TO FIND ORGANIZATIONS WITH SIMILAR RISK PROFILES. NOW COMPARE INTEREST RATES ACROSS THE PLATFORMS.

WHO ARE THE CHEAPEST?

WHY MIGHT THIS BE THE CASE?

MIXED

As the name suggests, this type of platform offers the applicant a mix of models. Generally, these tend to be a combination of reward and one other model.

Generally, campaigns opt for one model or another, but occasionally, one model might fail and the management opts to campaign using a different model. Or it may have, as part of its strategy, the aim of opening in one model and then transferring to another model for a second phase.

FOR EXAMPLE:

Campaign 'XYZ' opens phase one of its strategy with a reward model raise. This succeeds and the target is reached. Phase two is an equity raise to scale up the project and perhaps move into new geographical areas.

A huge advantage for project XYZ is that it has already engaged with a community and gained a following for its project. The management can then use this to help them spread the word and reach out to even more of the crowd as it begins stage two.

This kind of strategy will need a lot of planning but a big advantage is that the crowd may be able to offer some feedback on the project before stage two opens. With this kind of knowledge, the campaign should be in a much stronger position by the time stage two opens for business.

One of the biggest issues with the mixed model is communicating a cohesive vision across the different campaigns. Each model has a defined set of motivations for crowdconsent (see p48) to be given. Producing this cohesive message and communicating it across campaigns and communities is much more problematic than having just one message on which to focus. An advantage, though, is the ability, when the message is right, to move a tribe (or community) with the campaign from one platform/model to another.

TASK 5: MIXED MODEL

WHAT ARE THE ADVANTAGES AND DISADVANTAGES FOR YOUR CAMPAIGN OF USING A MIXED MODEL?

1.3

CROWDFUNDING'S DARK SIDE

Crowdfunding, at present, attracts some very positive coverage in the media with growth figures expected to explode in the next few years both in terms of numbers of platforms and the quantity of money loaned through them.

Do you have an idea for a project? Put the project 'out there' and let the masses come forth and fund it. This seems to be the popular mantra of the moment. It is often seen as a Utopian method of raising sufficient money for an opportunity to take flight, or at least start speeding down a runway.

For the most part, crowdfunding is a great way of attracting funding. It is a democratic method that connects project's managers with their potential customers. However, as with most good things in life, there may be downsides too.

This section aims to expose the darker (or riskier) sides of crowdfunding you may want to consider. Campaigns, like people, are unique, so not everything in this section will apply to every campaign.

By taking the 12 areas below into consideration, applicants should be able to make better judgments about the usefulness of crowdfunding to a project. My goal in writing this section is to help with planning the project and the campaign. After all, once you put it out into the public domain, you and your campaign will be exposed to critics from all sectors with all kinds of different opinions and, possibly, hidden agendas.

CARDS ON THE TABLE

Your idea may be very special, but using crowdfunding platforms to broadcast an idea to the crowd means you are, in effect, giving away the 'nuts and bolts' of what you want to do. Bear in mind that a competitor might see the idea, add to it, and do something even more special than you are planning.

This could apply to acrobatics just as much as to technology or zoos. Imagine you have a piece of theatre and you put it out there for crowdfunding, then lo and behold, a competitor in another part of the country suddenly does something very similar but with a little twist.

HOW WOULD YOU FEEL? WHAT COULD YOU DO?

If you take the decision to challenge this via legal channels, you will have to pay for this. How are you going to do this and how can you prove your competitor stole your idea? This can be a very tricky and potentially expensive problem.

IP ON THE TABLE

You may also have to expose something that has not yet completed the intellectual property process. Patents take time to file and complete, even a simple trademark in the UK takes three months to be granted and that's with no problems.

So before you start your crowdfunding campaign, think long and hard about how much you are going to tell potential investors about any IP you hold or are potentially going to hold. It may be worth holding off until you are on a more sure footing.

BUSINESS MODEL ON THE TABLE

Likewise, you may not want to show your business model to the world just yet. It could be that you have something really special. Perhaps you have used an existing model in a creative way; added to one to fashion something new; or even thought of something unique. Either one of these could be an advantage for any potential competitor if they were to gain insights into your thinking before you hit the market.

TIME TO CAMPAIGN

This is really about the opportunity costs of running a campaign in crowdfunding. A good campaign takes a lot of time and effort and needs to be carefully crafted before it can be put before a discerning crowd for inspection. This means you have even less of an already precious resource - your time!

Planning needs to be thorough, to ensure you are ready to hit the campaign trail, but what about the marketing plan that was due yesterday? Or the business plan you wanted to get ready before that talk at your local civic centre? Or even prepare the talk; when are you going to have time to write that before the campaign starts?

I am sure you get the picture; time is a reluctant friend to any project in most sectors, so getting this element right is really important.

TIME TO TALK (OR NOT)

Depending on the crowdfunding model you choose to use, it may be that you have to accommodate a large number of stakeholders in your project. These stakeholders will inevitably have varying degrees of knowledge about the project and the sector it is in. This may well mean yet more time will be taken up discussing details with stakeholders, reassuring them, and persuading them that you are in control and have taken into consideration all sides of the arguments put forward.

Crowdfunding also means that traditional means of raising funds for a start-up or for growth in an existing organization is changing. This could be seen as a good thing as the traditional 'gatekeepers' are swept aside in the rush to crowdfund, but bear in mind there was a reason these people existed. Venture capitalists and business angels had the potential to bring a lot of experience with them. They not only helped financially but also had contacts and know-how that money may not buy. Experience is one of the crucial things these individuals were able to offer, alongside any pecuniary help.

TAXING ISSUES

For all projects, a further layer of complication may be in the tax arrangements of the organization. Crowdfunding does not represent 'free' money. As with any income to an organization you need to declare it to your tax authority.

Depending on the country in which you are based, this income may be taxed and thus will add a further issue to the tax assessment you need to complete. Either way, it would be wise to double-check the arrangements in your specific country, as to the need to tell a taxing authority and then, of course, pay what is due.

ACCOUNTING FOR THINGS

Things may grow even more complicated if investors want to know details of your financial situation. This can take the form of simple requests about your trading figures for an existing organization or for more complicated information concerning the assets and the distribution of ownership in the organization.

Again, the biggest issue here is not so much the information required as the time that may be needed to collate it and then compose a logical and coherent message. Even then, there are no guarantees that the person requesting this information will actually invest in you, your team or the project.

Furthermore, do you really want to give away everything in your response? Projections and cash flows are something we advise never to reveal in full. It could be that a potential competitor is seeking to understand a possible new entry into their space; handing them this information could prove fatal for your opportunity.

RISKY YOUNG THINGS

Investors may want to know that they are protected. To ensure this, they may wish you to use some asset (for example, intellectual property rights or machinery) as collateral against their investment. If things go wrong they at least have something for their time and effort.

What about you? You could be left not only with dented pride but also the loss of the very thing you need to keep your project going. You might even have to start all over again from scratch - would you be happy to do that?

Checking the terms and conditions of the platform may help you in this situation. If you cannot find the relevant information, ask the platform for clarity.

RISKIER YOUNG THINGS

There is also the risk of you being taken to court if you tell untruths or exaggerate things to make the offer look better than it is. I have attended plenty of networking events where people sip their teas and coffees while lying about how well they are doing. In these situations, we really want the world to feel good about both the project and the management behind it (ourselves). So an extra zero inserted here or there, or the tale of a fictional contract or commission on the horizon, does nobody any harm, right? Well, wrong, actually.

If an investor relies on your provision of information and later finds this information was deceitful or incorrect, whether intended or not, they may have grounds to ask for recompense. Most things legal do not just come at a cost, they often come at a hefty cost.

It is better to tell it how it is and be honest from the outset. Crowdfunding is built on transparency; if a campaign seems opaque, in any way, it will generally struggle to gain support.

YOU ARE THE ONE

Failure is not a great feeling, failing in public through a crowdfunding campaign (everyone can see your performance) might be even worse.

You may be confident you gave it your best shot, but you still have to face friends, colleagues and partners. Worse may come as journalists and researchers start to pester you for interviews. Do you have the will to pick yourself up and put on a brave face for all these people?

Pre-crowdfunding might be a major source of help if you are unsure about any aspect of the campaign. Pre-crowdfunding works by allowing you the space to test a campaign, and gain vital feedback, before it goes live and asks for the money. The value pre-crowdfunding can add to any campaign is tremendous and it can help prevent some really silly mistakes while also creating 'buzz' around a campaign before it even launches.

EQUITY WORRIES

A crowd's understanding of equity is perhaps the biggest concern for government here in the UK. Understanding and education are the key issues concerning government.

Equity is, by nature, quite a high-risk gamble. It can be very rewarding and the economic payback quite substantial, but equally, investors can lose a lot of money taking equity in a small organization.

As we saw in 1.2 (equity) earlier, this is where the investor buys, or takes a share in, the organization. This share is not going to grow unless the organization grows. So the organization must be sold, split up and sold, floated on the stock market or a buyer must be found for the share the investor holds before they can liquidate (sell or exchange) their stake in the organization.

These are 'big asks' of any organization and, for this reason, the government wants to be sure that potential investors understand the risks before they put money into an equity share of an organization. One method of ensuring these risks are understood is to test the investor with a multiple-choice questionnaire. Get the answers right and the government and the crowdfunding platforms have at least satisfied themselves that the investor understands the fundamental risks involved.

FRAUD

Fraud is not a major concern to the platforms - yet. In the US, there have been several attempts to defraud the crowd. One of these attempts, *MYTHIC: The Story of Gods and Men*[17], a game that appeared on the Kickstarter platform in 2012, has been widely cited as a scam (although others think it may have been a hoax). No matter whether it was a hoax (essentially a joke) or a scam (trying to rip people off) there were some blatant attempts at copyright infringement by the creators of the game.

The game, launched on 24 April 2012, was attempting to raise $80,000, and was originally to run for 45 days (until 10 June 2012). Questions from the crowd were almost immediate and five questions were asked on day one of the campaign.

On 27 April, three responses to the questions were posted by the campaign's management team, Little Monster Productions (LMP). But on 28 April – just two days after the launch – two comments were posted that indicated, quite strongly, that this was a possible fraud.

This involved the following four points:

1. The concept art was thought to be stolen from a competitor
2. The character art work was thought to be stolen from another creator
3. The Facebook page (which had been removed) had pictures of an office that was thought to belong to another organization
4. No record was traceable of the business (LMP) having ever existed

This shows just how quickly the crowd was able to identify the suspicious elements of this campaign and were then able to pass along these suspicions to the rest of the crowd. This project was cancelled on 28 April 2012. It serves well as a point of interest for the industry and also for training providers like minivation.

Really, the point of this is that the crowd was policing the campaign and raised awareness of the potential for this campaign to be either a hoax or a scam. A total of 83 people offered to back the campaign – even after the suspicions were raised by two people on 28 April 2012 – just two days after the launch.

The first person to raise the issue provided the crowd with much-needed detail and links to prove his point. On the same day, another person, Christopher Michael Casey, also identified the potential for the game to be a scam after his research using the search engine Google - he found no evidence that the company behind the project existed and so came to the same conclusion as the first person who questioned it. Casey had pledged $1 to be able to access the comments section and communicate his findings. Do you think this added more weight to his claim? After all, he was prepared to lose a dollar to tell the crowd of his findings.

This is also the main thrust of the debate about fraud in crowdfunding; should the authorities and the platforms take a more proactive stance or can the crowd be relied on to sift through all the information about projects and identify problems? Or do we need a middle way that would involve the authorities, platforms and the crowd in governing the campaigns and checking they are what they report to be?

The debate continues, but in the UK, two trade bodies have already begun to address these issues and it is always worth ensuring that the platform you choose is a member of a recognized body. This simply means the platform has agreed to a minimum standard of operating principles and it also adds a layer of protection for you as campaign management and, of course, for the crowd adding value to your project.

Currently in the UK these two bodies are:

- p2p Finance Association[11] (focus on the interest model)
- UK Crowdfunding Association[12] (focus on crowdfunding generally)

But as the market expands and more niches are filled with crowdfunding, it is very likely that more of these will soon emerge and offer protection.

TASK 6: FRAUD

THINK FOR A MOMENT ABOUT THE MYTHIC GAME.

DO YOU THINK IT COULD HAVE BEEN A SCAM OR A HOAX? WHY?

SHOULD THE AUTHORITIES OR THE CROWD PLAY A MORE PROACTIVE ROLE IN POLICING CROWDFUNDING?

WHAT ARE THE GREATEST RISKS FOR YOUR VISION IN CROWDFUNDING?

DO THESE RISKS CHANGE ACCORDING TO DIFFERENT MODELS?

1.4

CAMPAIGN

In crowdfunding the term campaign is often used to describe the short-term activity of attracting funders. This is applicable to all models in the project finance path. But the term itself can be a little bit misleading. Most people probably think of a political, marketing or military campaign, rather than a crowdfunding campaign.

In order to define what we mean by a 'campaign' in this context we can turn to Alan Barnard and Chris Parker, two political campaign veterans, who offer the following concise definition:

"(A campaign is) a planned sequence of communications that makes use of all appropriate channels to achieve defined outcomes in a specific timeframe by influencing the decision–makers who will allow success."[18]

Ultimately, this is about influencing one party to agree to an action that the campaign management desires. This is achieved by communicating the benefits and the value to the crowd. Campaigning can be both an ethical or unethical activity depending on your perspective of the issues involved.

According to England's National Council for Voluntary Organisations, campaign activities can include a very wide range of activities and purposes and there also exist a wide range of definitions of the verb 'to campaign'. Broadly speaking, there are two fundamental reasons for campaigning: to maintain the status quo; or to change a situation. This can be achieved by employing all or any of the following activities:

- Boycotting products for political, ethical or environmental reasons
- Contacting and/or presenting your views to a local councillor, MP or targeted group
- Signing or starting a petition
- Taking an active part in, or lobbying as, a political campaign
- Taking part in a demonstration, a march, a picket or a strike
- Writing content for a recognized and widely read source

This list is relevant because a crowdfunding campaign is seeking permission to maintain and/or change the status quo. It is looking for approval for a project to begin or to grow. For campaign management, the context must be given due consideration.

From our work at the coalface we have developed a better definition of a crowdfunding campaign. Building on all these insights, campaigning in the crowdfunding context can be thought of as:

"A planned set of broadcasts that aim to motivate the crowd into adding value to a project within a given timeframe"

Communication is key to any campaign. Clear and understandable communication is vital and this communication must be conducted, at regular intervals, throughout the life of the campaign with all stakeholders. There are three stages to the planning of a successful campaign: pre-campaign, live campaign and post-campaign. All these stages must be carefully crafted together to produce a cohesive and coherent campaign.

Essentially, this is about timing. Each communication must be delivered with a message that is consistent with the campaign. There must be uniformity in the delivery of the message across channels. From emails, to campaign pages, to social media, the feel must not change. This is branding your message so that consistency is maintained throughout.

Crowdfunding is not an easy funding route. It needs precision in strategic planning (see 1.6, p81) that includes all aspects of the message you are using to attract the crowd's interest and get their consent to fulfil your aims. We call this *crowdconsent*.

A campaign for the crowdfunding project manager (the applicant) is not necessarily about maintaining the status quo, but rather about developing (including the possibility of growth) a certain project that will create value. By tapping into the potential of the crowd, applicants are generating interest in their project converting interest into action to help make the project become a reality. It may be that they want to create a small and sustainable ripple of interest that grows into a tsunami of interest, with significant media attention. Ideally, they would like the product or service, and the campaign, to go viral and reach a global audience (as we saw with Giacomo Sardelli at the very beginning of this book, even though for him it was a pleasant and well-deserved surprise).

In either scenario, good management is essential. Sticking to the original plan, while allowing for incremental adjustments, can be difficult. It can be challenging, in a small community-focused campaign, to stay the course with a plan and not lose sight of values, but this is important. Campaigns are a chance to share an opportunity with an audience, but the campaign values must fit those of the audience and those of the campaign managers. It should be a nutrient that nourishes stakeholders, not a toxin, poisoning them.

If it is to be a nutrient, there are essentially two ingredients that must be present in the mix for the campaign to succeed: trust and a clear message. Trust is about being credible to the crowd in terms of the message being conveyed. The message itself must be well articulated and communicated at a level that can be understood by the crowd.

These two elements need to be carefully blended to produce something that is credible and also clearly understood. The two elements should support each other in all communications the campaign produces.

A clear campaign message is necessary but, unless it seems trustworthy, the message will not be believed by the audience which, applicants hope, will help make the campaign a reality. Campaign content can undermined if it is poorly conveyed.

Aiming high in terms of both trust and message should result in crowdfunding campaigns that have much better chance of succeeding because they will:

a) Use confident language that is appropriate to the campaign
b) Provide facts and figures that underpin the believability of the campaign
c) Allow the values of the campaigns creators and audience to tally

Developing this concept further, and applying this to a visual framework, provides a clear set of nine positions into which a campaign may fit, depending on the depth of the research the applicant has conducted and the clarity of the message presented at all contact points with potential funders.

FIGURE 1.4.1: CROWDFUNDING'S NINE CAMPAIGN POSITIONS.

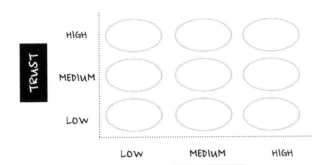

In creating this classification, the emphasis is on the existence of degrees of trust and communicability and is not a reflection of how successfully the campaign is likely to access funding from the crowd. It has been seen many times that, although a campaign may not be well communicated, it still reaches its targets. But it may also mean that the campaign will struggle to gain traction.

If, for example, a campaign is in the 'missing message' category, it may still reach its target, but its journey there may be a little more challenging than, say, a campaign that fits the 'medium middle' category.

A campaign can be a mix of these categories or even move between them. A classic example is when the management of a campaign add additional information clarifying a point raised by the crowd. This might be the key to adding clarity to the campaign and, in consequence, the campaign now reaches its targets with more traction than previously.

This is a generalization as every campaign is different; these categories simply add a guide note to help with analysis. But as crowdfunding is still very much in its infancy, it is useful to be able to compare and contrast these elements and have a benchmark (no matter how vague) to use in this analysis.

The summary in figure 1.4.1 adds much greater detail to the nine profiles and may help you determine where your campaign sits in the overall scheme of all things crowdfunded. Remember, though, that a perfect fit with any one of these categories is unlikely and it is often the case that a campaign has elements of more than one of these categories.

Nonetheless, the detail below serves well to help define the type of campaign you are creating and which ones you should try to avoid.

The details for the nine profiles are:

TABLE 1.4.1: CROWDFUNDING'S NINE CAMPAIGN POSITIONS DETAILED

TRUST	MESSAGE → LOW	MEDIUM	HIGH
HIGH	TRUSTED TRUSTEE IS WHERE THE FUNDER CAN BELIEVE IN THE PROJECT'S MANAGEMENT AND THE WORTHINESS OF THE CAMPAIGN BUT THE WAY THE MESSAGE IS CONVEYED LETS THE CAMPAIGN DOWN	TRUSTED COHESIVE IS WHERE THE CAMPAIGN SHOWS STRONG RESEARCH AND IS BELIEVABLE IN TERMS OF ITS VISION AND FEASIBILITY. HOWEVER, THERE MAY BE MISALIGNMENTS WITH THE CAMPAIGN'S MESSAGES	MISSION OF LOVE IS THE CAMPAIGN MOST LIKELY TO BECOME A REALITY BECAUSE IT IS FOUNDED ON EVIDENCE AND ITS MESSAGES ARE DELIVERED CONVINCINGLY. IT IS COHESIVE, COHERENT AND VALUE CAN BE RECOGNIZED BY ALL STAKEHOLDERS
MEDIUM	MISSING MESSAGE IS A CAMPAIGN THAT INSPIRES SOME TRUST IN ITS VISION AND WORTHINESS BUT LACKS CLARITY IN TERMS OF ITS MESSAGE. SOME FACTUAL INFORMATION MAY BE MISSING OR WRONG	MEDIUM MIDDLE HAS AN AVERAGE MESSAGE WITH SOME BELIEVABLE ELEMENTS TO THE CAMPAIGN'S VISION. IT IS VITAL THE MESSAGE IS COHESIVE OTHERWISE THE CAMPAIGN RISKS SLIPPING DOWN THIS PROFILE OUTLINE	MISSING MISSION HAS A STRONG MESSAGE CONVEYED IN A COHESIVE AND COHERENT MANNER, BUT THE REALITY OF THE VISION MAY NOT BE SHARED BY THOSE FROM WHOM THE CAMPAIGN IS SEEKING PERMISSION
LOW	ANTIPATHY IS THE LEAST POSITIVE PROFILE. THE MESSAGE LACKS COHERENCY AND COHESIVENESS, THE VISION IS UNCLEAR AND TRUST IN THE CAMPAIGN IS VERY LOW	MIXED MESSAGE IS NOT READILY UNDERSTOOD BY THE CROWD. A MESSAGE IN THIS CATEGORY CAN BE ARTICULATED FAIRLY CLEARLY BUT IS OPEN TO MISINTERPRETATION. THIS IS COUPLED WITH LOW LEVELS OF TRUST IN THE CAMPAIGN VISION	MISSION IMPOSSIBLE IS WHEN THE MESSAGE IS CLEAR BUT IT DOES NOT INSPIRE TRUST OR APPEAR CREDIBLE. THIS COULD BE TRUST IN THE MANAGEMENT, IN THE VISION OR IN BOTH

TASK 7: RESEARCH CAMPAIGN PROFILES

FIND A REPRESENTATIONAL EXAMPLE ONLINE THAT FITS ONE OF THE NINE POSITIONS OUTLINED ABOVE.

TRY TO FIND A CAMPAIGN THAT IS SIMILAR TO THE ONE YOU WANT TO START.

PROFILE THAT CAMPAIGN AND IDENTIFY THE STRENGTHS AND THE WEAKNESSES IN THAT CAMPAIGN. ON REFLECTION – ASK YOURSELF WHAT HAVE I LEARNED?

Crowdfunding campaigns are about moving the audience to action. Without the action of the crowd, the campaign will fail and the opportunity will be wasted. Thus communication with the crowd must reinforce the story being told, no matter what channel of communication is used. That story must be accurate (truthful) and consistent across all channels.

It is often said that "people buy from people" and the same can be said for crowdfunding: people back people. There is research that suggests that geography that used to be so important for start-up projects seeking funding from a business angel or even a bank, is no longer as relevant.[19]

Friends and family investing early in a project helps send signals to more geographically-remote funders that the project is worth backing. The signal says: "Hey, look at us, we know something you don't and have acted on that knowledge by backing this project." People further away rely on this kind of information. Once they see it, they may act in the belief that they are following good and trustworthy information. This difference in information held by the crowd is called *asymmetrical information*.

Often, traditional investors relied on the personality of the entrepreneur behind the project. This could be assessed by meeting the entrepreneur face to face; however with the huge distances that often now exist between the funder and the applicant, this is no longer the case. Signals given out by the project's early funders are important aspects of a campaign reaching its target.

This means the communication of the campaign must be even more compelling, to attract these distant funders. Naturally, the better the communication and the more credible the story, the better the chances of gaining approval from the crowd and action being taken. We call this crowdconsent – because actually this is exactly what you are attempting to gain: the consent of the crowd to enable you to realize your vision.

The campaign DREIM model (Donation, Reward, Equity, Interest and Mixed), action is still the desired outcome and this is why the campaign needs to move the crowd into responding to the message. But the message has to be appropriate and ethical. Fraudulent campaigns damage the industry's and stakeholders' reputation. Fortunately, as we read in section 1.3, we live in a highly connected world and the likelihood of a fraudulent campaign succeeding is extremely low. Crowds are prepared to conduct research and broadcast their findings. Problems, of course, arise when these findings are incomplete or inaccurate and conclusions are drawn from them that may be wrong. But on the whole, crowds have proven quite effective at raising issues and investigating concerns.

Responding to the crowd's concerns can also help alleviate some of the concerns the crowd may have. In most platforms, a Q&A board (or a comments section) is an established method of asking the applicant questions. Personal emails may also be exchanged to clarify points or indeed make offers beyond the campaign.

Applicants must respond to the crowd promptly, no matter which method of response they choose. Sometimes, the simplest of questions can turn out to have the most impact if it is not handled correctly. Campaign management must be prepared to listen to funders'(and potential funders') views and concerns; after all, by posing questions that need to be answered, they may actually help the management to present their campaign better.

The golden rule is never to ignore any questions. Questions are the oxygen in the blood of the campaign because questions mean the management is engaging with the crowd. Once the crowd is engaged, it may only take a small nudge for consent to be given and action taken.

But why would an applicant want to ignore the questions from the crowd anyway? The management has a responsibility to the crowd and other stakeholders in the campaign to produce an ethical message that will move the crowd to action. This involves two-way communication from the outset. So when planning the campaign, it is vital to take this aspect into consideration (including the time it will take to craft a response).

No crowdfunding campaign operates in a vacuum; it is likely that it will be competing with other campaigns in similar areas, maybe looking for similar segments of the crowd, so any questions that are raised about the campaign, from either the crowd or competing campaigns, must be handled with care. Ranting and raving behind the scenes is fine, but never allow this into the public sphere.

Emotional intelligence is sometimes called for when responding to questions from the public domain. Criticism of a project can be hard to take but it must be handled well. Most crowdfunding communication will be in the public domain, so this is not the place to put down any individual asking questions. Neither is it the place for criticizing other campaigns.

Applying emotional intelligence involves appearing calm and collected (at least on the outside) in all your communications and dealings in the public domain. For example, we always thank individuals for their questions and try to address their concerns as directly as possible.

For applicants, the crowd is also an element of the strategic analysis that needs careful consideration. Ask yourself "who are the most likely people to give consent?"

Knowing this is pretty important for the management team as it can plan more direct communications with these sections of the crowd. By tailoring the message of the campaign more precisely, applicants may inspire action by this target audience within the crowd and it will be easier to track and measure this accurately.

It should also be remembered that the target audience of the campaign may shift over the duration of the live phase. This is because the questions and responses may highlight different levels of value for different segments of the crowd.

Different groups will also give their consent at different phases of a campaign. It can be tricky predicting when this might happen, but trying to calculate when they should be called to action is important because it provides some indication of possible patterns that the campaign may follow.

A useful way of managing this aspect of the campaign is to decide early on who will be the primary, secondary and tertiary targets (see 2.2, p110). The challenge continues, as once these targets are identified, the applicant needs to work out at what point in the campaign's life cycle they are likely to give their consent.

To maximize impact, once action from the first group has been generated, it is time to move on to the second group and so on until all segments have provided their consent. These predictions should be based on sound evidence.

The worst thing a management team can do is to try and second-guess the motivations or the timings of a campaign without thorough research. More discussion of these issues will be provided in section 2.

In extreme cases, questions from any side of the crowdfunding relationship may change the perspective of the campaign. This may not be due to bad planning on the part of management but rather because new insights are gained that could not have been foreseen; or perhaps the context changes in the external environment resulting in some shift in the political or social landscape. For these reasons, campaigns should have a degree of flexibility built into their structure to allow them to adapt to changing circumstances and problems that may arise.

STEEPLED

In order to get a better idea of issues that might impact the campaign and the crowdconsent applicants are seeking, conduct a STEEPLED analysis.

STEEPLED is an acronym that stands for the following:

- Social-cultural
- Technological
- Economic
- Environmental
- Political
- Legal
- Educational
- Demographic

Campaigns do not end with the raise (getting the money). Crowdfunding is really the beginning of a journey with those who have provided consent to the project. By looking at the various elements that can affect a campaign and the business model behind it, management will be much stronger and will have taken much deeper risks into consideration before its launch.

This type of analysis can really help when tricky questions are asked by the crowd. You may have already thought through the problem the crowd presents in its questions and already have an answer to hand because a STEEPLED analysis has been conducted.
This is the real strength of this kind of analysis, it can help identify risks for management, and enable plans to be put in place to lessen their impact. Though, of course, not every risk to which the campaign is exposed will be addressed in this analysis - and nor will all the questions that can be asked by the crowd.

There will be issues and questions that are, at times, difficult to answer. There may even be sensitive issues that are uncomfortable to address or issues that you do not want to reveal. That is fine when addressing the crowd; however for internal strategy purposes, these issues need to be addressed and should begin to be thought about (or even emerge) with the STEEPLED analysis.

The simplest way to approach a STEEPLED analysis is to ask questions related to the opportunity that are focused on each aspect of the acronym. The questions do not need to be very deep and can even seem a little superficial at times.

Not all the aspects of the STEEPLED analysis need to be covered either. It will depend on your business model and the campaign. For example, a campaign and business opportunity related to care homes for the elderly may be more concerned with demographic questions than with educational ones. Likewise, a beer producer might be equally concerned with these aspects and less so with political questions.

A generic example of questions is given in table 1.4.2:

TABLE 1.4.2: GENERIC EXAMPLE OF STEEPLED ANALYSIS

ASPECT	QUESTIONS
SOCIAL-CULTURAL	WHAT TRENDS ARE LIKELY TO IMPACT THE CAMPAIGN?
TECHNOLOGICAL	WHAT TECHNOLOGICAL CHANGES ARE LIKELY IN THE NEXT FEW YEARS?
ECONOMIC	IS THE ECONOMY STABLE? WHAT PREDICTIONS ARE THERE FOR THE NEXT FEW YEARS?
ENVIRONMENTAL	HOW COULD WE LESSON OUR IMPACT? WHAT CAN WE DO AND WHAT EFFECTS WILL THIS HAVE?
POLITICAL	WHAT LOCAL AND NATIONAL CHANGES ARE LIKELY IN THE NEXT FEW YEARS?
LEGAL	ARE THERE ANY LEGISLATIVE AREAS THAT ARE OF CONCERN TO THE CAMPAIGN?
EDUCATIONAL	WHAT EDUCATIONAL OPPORTUNITIES ARE THERE OR CAN WE PROVIDE?
DEMOGRAPHIC	ARE THERE ANY SIGNIFICANT CHANGES PREDICTED – HOW DOES THIS SITUATION IMPACT THE CAMPAIGN?

This table can be tailored to be more relevant to any campaign. The focus here is the external environment and how changes (or even things remaining the same) in these areas can impact the campaign (and also the community that is being engaged through the campaign).

As stated earlier, this will not eliminate all risks but it will help to make them more manageable and eliminate some unforeseen events impacting the progress of the campaign. The best way to produce this type of analysis is to involve all team members and gain feedback from a broad range of people before going live.

TASK 8: STEEPLED

CREATE A STEEPLED ANALYSIS FOR YOUR CAMPAIGN.

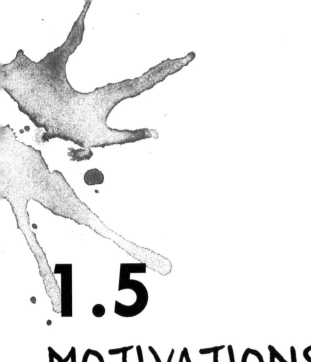

1.5

MOTIVATIONS

We begin this section with a task:

TASK 9: WHY?

WRITE AT LEAST ONE PAGE OF A4 ANSWERING THE QUESTION:
"WHY AM I PLANNING A CAMPAIGN?"

By starting a campaign you are making an effort to add value to your future as well as the future of others. This is a special situation demanding some special time. If the campaign is successful it will give something back, maintain something, or change something (perhaps by preventing an alternative course of action). If successful, this campaign is about to add value to a future that you and your team members have envisaged.

A crowdfunding campaign takes a lot of energy and will require long hours of planning, processing and producing. These three Ps are critical in that they cover the temporal elements of a campaign (before, during and after). This is why it is important to understand the basics and to be able to write a page about why you are planning a campaign, with honesty.

What this really means is that the applicant must be prepared to give the campaign 100% of their attention. Applicants should not expect to succeed if they enter the campaign half-heartedly, the campaign exists to create a vision that the campaign applicant wants (or needs) to achieve. But does the applicant have the will to see the campaign through to the end?

In answer to this last question, the simple response must be "yes"; if it is not a firm "yes" then don't do it (yet).

Bear in mind that 56% of projects fail on Kickstarter alone.[20] Presuming this figure is even remotely accurate, this serves to demonstrate that campaigns need to be properly organized and planned before they go live to the public. This planning should also include getting your close friends and family on board from the very beginning. There is some evidence that the earlier your strong ties (close friends and family members) are seen to fund a project, in the project finance model, the better its chances of success. It sends out a clear message to observant weak ties (friends of friends or friends of family members) that the project is worth backing.

It is interesting to note that this is in direct contrast with the findings of Zhang and Liu.[21] These researchers were looking at the personal finance path and observed the opposite effect. The more funders herded (mass movement by the crowd) irrationally toward a campaign, the less likely it was to maintain the momentum and thus reach its funding target. It must be remembered though that the crowd is bidding the interest rates down in this model and so savvy investors will seek higher returns elsewhere when they see the crowd moving en-masse (herding) towards a loan. They know they can get better rates elsewhere and so opt to look at other requests possibly on alternative platforms. See table 1.5.1 for a comparison.

TABLE 1.5.1: HERDING EFFECTS IN EQUITY AND INTEREST MODELS

EQUITY MODEL	EARLY HERDING A POSITIVE
INTEREST MODEL	EARLY HERDING A NEGATIVE

Motivations are generally different for the applicant and the funder. These motivations also change depending on the individual and their background circumstances as well as the model being used to campaign for the vision. Listed below are some general motivational factors starting with the funder:

Motivational factors for funders; they get the chance to:
- 'Invest' in projects with a suitable risk profile
- Support a project with passion
- Participate at new levels
- Understand the process
- Be an investor
- Gain value or ROI (return-on-investment)
- Have fun

Motivational factors for applicants:
- Combination of funding channels or single focus funding channel
- Able to offer a reward
- Feedback on projects
- Public attention
- Raising money
- Low costs

SOCIAL ELEMENT

There may be other factors that I have not identified here that are applicable to your campaign. Niche fulfilment, for example, might be another motivating factor for either the funder or the applicant. Once again, it depends on the campaign and the vision that is being created and the language being used in that communication.

In a 2014 academic study by Tanushree Mitra and Eric Gilbert,[22] language use in crowdfunding was considered from a much deeper perspective. These academics developed a list of the key phrases that helped gain funding and those that did not. The study focused on campaigns on the platform Kickstarter and what they found supported a long known, but little researched area of crowdfunding. They confirmed there were are five essential elements that seem to act as a motivators for the crowd:

- Authority
- Liking
- Reciprocity
- Scarcity
- Social proof

Authority is really about power. You trust someone that you believe is in a position of authority and thus able to guide you and add value for you via their acknowledged wisdom and learning.

Liking is a fundamental aspect of any interaction with other humans. We need to be liked and we trust people we like.

Reciprocity is another very fundamental human trait. We like to help others and we like to feel that we are helping others. Through gifting our knowledge or actions to aid others (especially those less fortunate than ourselves) we receive a warm glow as reward.

Scarcity: if things are scarce they tend to be valued more. Often this is actually about perception rather than reality. If things are perceived to be scarce or rare, people often want to be associated with, or to take possession of, them. For the crowd, this can work to a campaign's advantage. Highlighting the limited amount or number in a campaign (especially rewards) can be a wonderful motivating factor for crowdconsent.

Social proof is something with which most of us engage anyway (we may not realize this is what it is or what we are doing). This element boils down to fellow acknowledgement of our choices. Social proof is powerful because once others also add value to a campaign it provides you with the satisfactory knowledge that you were right to take action and offer your consent. Generally, the bigger the crowd that follows suit, the happier that individual is. In extreme examples, it can also mean masses moving in a certain direction because of the 'me too' factor of social proof, we call this *herding*.

At minivation, we would add two more to this list: commitment and consistency.

Commitment is related to social proof. Once individuals have publicly given their backing to a campaign they rarely back down unless they are given a legitimate reason to do so. An example would be backers asking questions to the management of a campaign and members of the crowd feeling that their answers were hiding something or not addressing the core issue they wanted addressed.

Consistency: consistent patterns of behaviour (and language use) by the applicant can help reinforce the commitment of funders. This is why so much planning goes into each campaign and why, as far as possible, things are planned in terms of what will be said in the updates and so on.

We will revisit the research of Mitra and Gilbert in section 3.7, where more detail of their findings are given.

CASE IN POINT

One of the fastest campaigns to succeed in 2012 was microco.sm[23] which took 15 hours in late November to raise £50,000 for a 10% stake on the Seedrs equity model platform. This achievement by the team at microco.sm was not by luck alone, nor was it down to the simplicity of them having a great product. In an interview with Seedrs CEO, Jeff Lynn, he revealed that the management team behind the campaign already had the investors interested and had been working for weeks beforehand to get them to agree to invest in the campaign when it went live. True to their word, the investors did so over the course of the 15 hours and microco.sm achieved their funding in record time.

Investors and applicant were motivated to reach their goals and see the project succeed. In reality though, most project managers will have little time to visit many potential funders before they go live. This is especially true in the craft sector where the organization may consist of just one person with little or no experience of raising finance for an entrepreneurial project.

Another area of support that should be into taken account when planning a campaign is the family and friends network upon which applicants can rely. During most projects there are going to be some dark moments when applicants feel like stopping the campaign early and calling off the whole thing. Family and friends can be a great source of support and comfort during these times, so make sure they are aware of the campaign early on and that you will need their support in terms of emotional motivation (as well as funding).

The number of Facebook 'friends' an applicant has appears to have an effect on campaign success.[24] The bigger your network on Facebook, the better your chances of campaign success. You will still need to send out regular reminders via email to move the conversion of the crowd out of passive observation and into active engagement.

In other words, the broadcasting of a campaign on social media sites like Facebook has an effect on the funding of the campaign by those in that particular social media network. However, this should be complemented by an email invitation to these same individuals in the network, asking them to contribute.

Two types of communication with individuals is required - one through the social media of choice and another via email. Email may be a little old school, but it cannot be ignored - there is a lot of evidence to suggest that it is still one of the most powerful ways to gain crowdconsent.

TASK 10: WHO?

HOW WILL YOU RECORD THE CONTACT DETAILS OF THOSE WHO CONTRIBUTE TO THE CAMPAIGN?

IF THE CAMPAIGN FAILS, HOW WILL YOU THANK THOSE THAT HAVE CONTRIBUTED?

One last thought for the applicant in terms of motivation. If the campaign fails, there may be an opportunity to try again in future. For this reason, think about how an applicant can reward those strong and weak ties who lent their support during this time. It is probably not expected by them, but something to say "thank you" will ensure goodwill for the future.

This could also be an opportunity to ask for their input as to why they think the campaign failed. It is possible that strong and weak ties have a very different perceptions of the reason for failure from the applicant. Lessons could be learned from this experience to inform any future campaigns.

TASK II: DETAILS

WORK OUT THE TIME YOU WILL NEED TO PLAN AND ORGANIZE YOUR CAMPAIGN.

NOW THINK ABOUT EARLY FUNDERS FOR THE CAMPAIGN. WHAT VALUE DOES EACH OF YOU GAIN FROM THIS RELATIONSHIP?

HOW MUCH TIME MIGHT YOU NEED TO PERSUADE THEM TO JOIN THE CAMPAIGN?

WHEN IN THE LIFE CYCLE OF THE CAMPAIGN WILL THEY GIVE CROWDCONSENT?

1.6

CAMPAIGN STRATEGY

"A good strategy has coherence, co-ordinating actions, policies, and resources so as to accomplish an important end."[25]

This summary by Richard Rumelt is brilliantly concise. It is also applicable to any applicant looking to crowdfund a project, no matter how small that project may be.

Coherence is needed for all stakeholders to understand the vision your campaign is trying to realize. Without coherence, the message that should be driving the campaign can be lost or misunderstood (see section 1.4).

It is necessary to co-ordinate actions to produce a unified look and feel to the project both internally for the project's team and externally for those wishing to follow and/or invest in the campaign. To help with this, written policies are needed (even for small-scale projects) setting out the guidelines and rules about how the project is to be managed. It takes time to develop and write a coherent set of guides, but the benefits are enormous as all team members will understand and work towards one vision.

Finally, the resources the applicant has at their disposal need to be considered and can include social media as well as more tangible resources. Planning the use of these resources will help to ensure maximum efficiency is achieved.

It should now be much clearer why the applicant of a small-scale project can benefit from having a concise strategy in place. It will help to develop a common set of goals in a coherent plan that all stakeholders can understand and follow.

But let's be honest, strategy, for most people outside the corporate world, is not something that helps us spring out of bed in the morning. An applicant reading this book has an advantage over most competing campaigns, because most competitors probably do not have a realistic strategic plan in place.

This is especially true of the smaller end of the creative industries where the business lexicon and traditional means of teaching entrepreneurship and its associated equations, facts and figures are often perceived quite negatively. For this reason alone it is perhaps of greater importance that the applicant of creative industry campaigns thinks, through the strategy that will lead to achieving goals.

Most funders will not need to see or hear about your strategy itself. For the most part, they care about impact. They want to know that their money is not going to be wasted and that the campaign will leave them safe in the knowledge that they have added value to a real project, devoid of any fraud.

How you planned and sweated over the campaign's exact details are not of concern to most funders. They are interested in the benefits the campaign brings, not in the functions of the unseen operations (the back office). Think of this as a stage performance. An audience only needs to see the lighting, the stage, the props and the actors and hear the sounds (including music) that have been pre-determined. It is not necessary for the audience to understand fully the stage manager's role, the front of house role or the myriad of other roles needed to put on a show.

These elements add greatly to the experience of the audience but their functions are hidden, not because the audience is unable or incapable of understanding these processes, but because their presence adds nothing of value to the audience's experience of the play.

But in reality, without this back office planning, the campaign is going to look and feel very clumsy and awkward. Chances of success are greatly reduced because the applicant and the team behind the campaign will have no idea where they are going at any particular point in the journey.

In essence, there are three main areas to think about, and these relate to our story-telling skills encountered in section 1.4. Any good story has a beginning, middle and end. The same applies to a crowdfunding campaign under any of the project models. The planning of the campaign should be based around the beginning, the middle and the end. In this way, the whole campaign will be much more cohesive and coherent in the context of the campaign's vision.

As previously mentioned, to help the applicant with this important stage, we have developed the Crowdfunding Planning Page. This is a very simple idea that will greatly aid the development of the campaign's strategy.

There are three sections across the top of the page representing:

- Pre-campaign (beginning)
- Live (middle)
- Post-campaign (end)

Across the bottom there are two boxes for:

- Pitch (beginning and middle)
- Promises (end)

Each of these elements will be given much more attention in their respective sections. What follows here is a brief introduction to the CPP and how it can help.

This tool can be downloaded and enlarged free from the minivation web site (www.minivation.org). Once this is done, sticky notes can be used in each section to detail the actions that are necessary for that section to be ready when the campaign goes live and finally finishes. Sticky notes are used as these can be altered at any time, scrapped or re-written.

As ideas are expanded and new ideas are added, so the sticky notes can be moved around the page. It is also unnecessary to use just text, images can sometimes prove much better when conveying an idea. Simple stick figures or star people can be used - you do not need to be a brilliant artist to use them on the CPP. But you do need to share your page, this will enable the team or even outsiders to add comments and make suggestions about your campaign structure before you go live.

Using sticky notes adds a degree of flexibility to the planning process and also allows for the development of ideas as the CPP becomes populated with content. Ideas often lead to other thoughts, so by keeping the CPP as flexible as possible, these ideas can easily be incorporated into the planning process.

For some people, setting a deadline for completing each of the sections is a way to maintain a degree of discipline in the planning stages. It may also help to designate each section to a team member for completion - the point being that there are many ways to use a CPP and each campaign has a unique combination of the different sections.

If you know of other campaigns being planned in different fields why not get together for a 'show and tell' session with the management of these other campaigns? It may be that solutions to campaign problems or scenarios can be found that would not have emerged by other means.

FIGURE 1.6.1: CROWDFUNDING PLANNING PAGE (CPP)

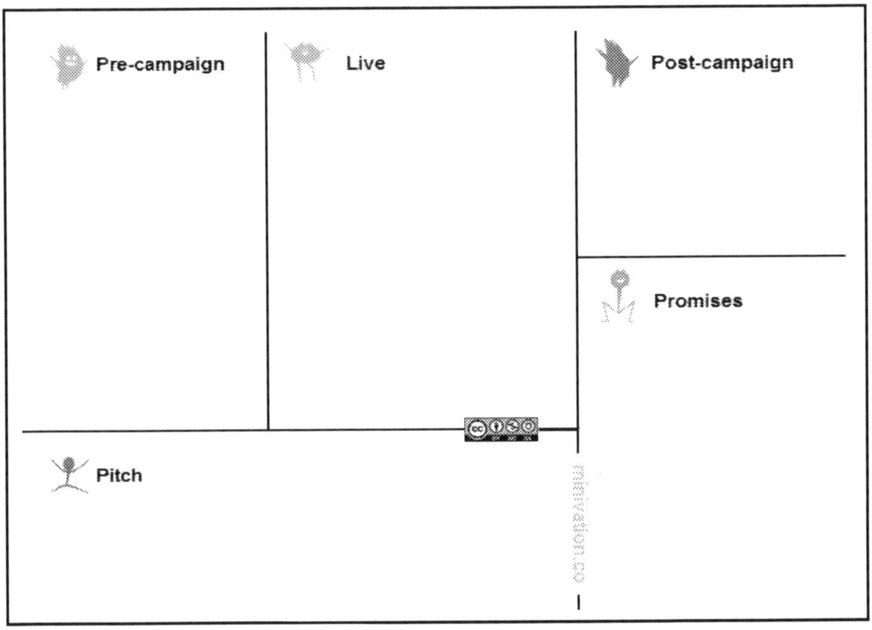

There is no right or wrong way to complete a CPP and it is intended to be developed and expanded as ideas are formed and included. Development of the CPP has been a long process and comes from the planning exercises we have done with many campaigns in many sectors. It works well with all models and in all fields.

As an agency, minivation has learned that the people who criticize campaigns the most are often the people who really want it to work. This is because they have a passion and desire for the project to create the value they are seeking. So if someone seems, at first, a little heavy-handed in the way they critique your CPP, step back and consider why.

If you draw the conclusion that actually they have a negative perception of the project, and you are sure they are a minority of the population, then try to put that criticism to one side and continue with your development of the strategy for the campaign. Often the harshest critics can become the loudest supporters. But for this to happen, both you and the critics have to believe in your campaign and the impact it is going to have.

1.7

PROJECT PLANNING

By now, it should be obvious that planning is essential. It may seem boring and applicants may want to head straight out there on the platform of their choice and start campaigning, but without careful pre-planning the campaign will find itself adrift in a sea of noise with no clear means of setting a course or even knowing the direction from which it has come (or is heading). Things to think about in the planning stages are:

VISION

Does the plan have a clear end result, a clear vision it is trying to achieve? It is easy to ignore this, but without a clear set of achievable aims and end objective the motivation of your team will start to wane, and once this happens, it won't be long before the same happens to your crowd. A clear vision helps keep everyone on track and success on their minds.

VALUES

The values of both the team and the aims of the project must match. It is vital that the team behind the campaign believes in the aims and believe these are achievable in the timeframe the campaign allows.

This also applies to your network (see below); it too needs to believe in the project.

NETWORK

Make sure all the potential funders of the campaign have been notified of the timeframe and are happy to invest through the platform within this window of opportunity. The network can be segmented into strong ties (friends and family), weak ties (colleagues and associates that may have been made through friends and family) and tertiary ties (those people with whom you have regular contact on social media but have never actually met, who have no physical connections with your strong or weak ties). These all play a vital role in giving the campaign traction.

CHANNELS

Make sure you make it clear to all stakeholders how they can expect to communicate with each other and the management. This also applies to the funders, make sure everyone in the team knows how and when communications are expected to happen with the fanbase the campaign will build and through which channels.

PROMISES

These must be acted upon and delivered when the campaign states this will happen. One of the biggest criticisms offered by crowdfunding sceptics is that, too often, rewards fail to materialize, are delivered late or are of inferior quality to that stated in the campaign. This is easily avoidable by not going over the top with the promises on offer. Scale it back and make them realistic and above all, be honest.

MEASUREMENT

How will the campaigns team know if they are on track?

Be clear about the milestones that are expected to be reached and when. This means being absolutely sure everyone in the team is communicating with one another when (and how) they should be. But prepare for the worst. If they are not, what will management do about the situation to get the campaign back on track?

Equally, be aware that there may be too much inefficient communication between team members or even stakeholders. There has to be a balance and, as each campaign is unique, so the balance is different in each scenario (see 2.1 and 3.2).

When the campaign goes live, the questions just mentioned are perhaps the most important ones for the campaign management team. Knowing where the campaign is, and where it was thought to be, will help when making strategic choices.

Choices have to be made in the life of any campaign, no matter how small or large. Crowdfunding is a social activity and one that demands strong communication skills to broadcast the value being created. But how do you measure the success of an individual communication or a full-blown communications strategy?

These are tough questions to answer. If a campaign is not reaching its targets what should you do? Start updating daily (or more) through all channels? Ease back on the communications or be more selective about the channels through which you update? Could you increase the quality of your communications? But then you need to think what do you mean by quality of communications? How can we measure this?

What if the campaign is a runaway success? What will you offer in the way of stretch goals (see section 3.3, p187) and what will you do to answer the hundreds of enquiries coming at you from the press, the platform and emails?

Either of these situations can be a real challenge for an experienced team, for those venturing into crowdfunding for the first time they can be overwhelming. The result in the latter situation is often what we, at minivation, call "bog frenzy".

When things really start to heat up a kind of panic sweeps through the management team and creates bog frenzy. People become incapable of following the basic rules laid down at the beginning and they start to react to crisis after crisis.

This situation now dominates the everyday activities of the team and they become paralyzed by this and temporarily incapable of doing anything other than react to the situation in front of them. Creativity of thought is suspended as issues in hand need addressing quickly leaving no time for thinking beyond the immediate tasks. The team is bogged down by the frenzy of activity released by the campaign - it is a victim of its own (temporary) success.

This is not so much a crisis but a build up of questions that can hit the team harder than expected. Far from being a crisis, we would argue this is the perfect place to be in when a campaign is trying to reach out to as many of the crowd members for their consent as possible. In short - it seems to be working!

More often than not the 'problem' is that teams have failed to set realistic milestones for the campaign and are caught off-balance when the campaign either hits the brakes and slows down or hits the accelerator and speeds up.

This is annoying because it does not have to be this way. A few simple steps can really help the campaign to stay on track and keep the traction balanced.

Success

For your campaign, what will success look like?

This is actually a deceptively simple question because the answer will be different for each campaign. Even team members in a campaign may not answer this question in the same way because the success of a campaign can be measured in many ways.

By default, most people think success in crowdfunding is a simple matter of getting the money. Actually there are several ways to measure success in crowdfunding, although it should be said that hitting the raise target is certainly a big one.

Success can be measured in many ways and even in combination with other criteria. Below is short list that demonstrates the point – any one of these could be the main criterion for measuring the success of your campaign:

- Money raised
- Time time to raise the target amount
- How many people 'like' the campaign or tweet about it
- Success in building the social network
- Getting into the press
- Engagement with the broader public
- Teaching and educating people about the project
- Helping those in need
- Delivering on time and to a set quality standard

There are many more which will be dependent on your campaign. Once you know what success will be, how it will look and feel, measurements can be taken to ensure the campaign is on track to meet these criteria.

CLARITY

Set the ground rules early. Responsibilities should be assigned and each member of the team must be clear about what these entail. Ensure members are able to question things in an open and frank manner. A campaign is a tricky balance to get right but with clearly-defined roles given to each team member, the campaign should run much more smoothly. When problems do arise, they can be solved in a timely manner with minimum fuss and disruption.

OPERATIONS

External partners may also be needed to help the campaign achieve its targets and fulfil the promises made. These partners must be aware of the critical timeframes by which you are expecting them to engage or deliver. For example, if you are having posters printed as a reward for funding, you need to ensure enough posters are being produced to meet the number of funders and that these are sent to the right recipients on time.

It might be an idea to get some kind of legally-binding agreement with the suppliers if the promises are being handled by an external partner. Realistically, though, few projects are going to be on a scale where this becomes problematic.

There are many tools available to the applicant for use when planning the project, but the CPP is perhaps one of the best starting places to think about the campaign and the overall aims it is trying to achieve. As we saw in section 1.6, the CPP will help the applicant set out their campaign strategy and reach their anticipated goals.

Developed specifically for crowdfunding, CPP is one of several tools that can be used in combination to help the applicant develop a much stronger sense of the aim and objectives they are attempting to achieve.

Other tools, including STEEPLED (see 1.4), SWOT and SMART, allow the applicant to first look at the macro environment and then to focus on the micro environment. In other words, the applicant can look at the external forces that may impact the campaign and then apply these to the internal workings of the campaign.

TIMELINES

The easiest way to start planning for this scenario is to create a simple timeline. A timeline is just as it sounds: a line drawn on a page with the start on one side and an end point at the other. Timelines are useful because they are simple to use and very visual. Especially if the line drawn is an arrow, this immediately indicates to the reader the direction time and the sequence of events will follow. A simple example is given below:

FIGURE 1.7.1: A SIMPLE TIMELINE IN THE SHAPE OF AN ARROW

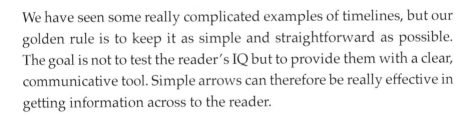

We have seen some really complicated examples of timelines, but our golden rule is to keep it as simple and straightforward as possible. The goal is not to test the reader's IQ but to provide them with a clear, communicative tool. Simple arrows can therefore be really effective in getting information across to the reader.

Of course, they can become more complicated as detail is added. This detail can be offshoots placed on either side of the arrow in the correct chronological order to demonstrate the needs of the project as time progresses, as illustrated on the next page:

FIGURE 1.7.2: SIMPLE TIMELINE WITH MILESTONES

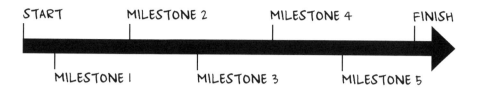

This straightforward example immediately provides the reader with an understanding of the five milestones, when they are likely to happen (the sequence) and the start/end dates (which can be added). It is uncluttered and to the point.

More detail can, of course, be added and the best way to do this is to build on the basic example by adding off-shoots to the text boxes with the numbered milestones. There will probably come a point where the simplicity of the timeline is lost as more and more information is added. For this reason, only add essential information to the timeline and make sure your team is aware of how the campaign is progressing in relation to this timeline.

Broadcasting this to the external crowd can also help the campaign. It can engage the crowd and thus motivate them into action. If things are not going to plan, why not ask the crowd for advice and suggestions on how to get the campaign back on track?

They might be able to see the answers you cannot!

PLANNING - SWOT ANALYSIS

Once a STEEPLED analysis is completed, a SWOT can be used to identify the Strengths, Weaknesses, Opportunities and Threats of the campaign and the business model. Using the answers to the questions already addressed in the STEEPLED analysis, a much deeper and more thought-provoking set of outlines for the campaign can be built.

A SWOT analysis is really about two important areas of a campaign: the internal and external environments. They can be divided up as demonstrated below in table 1.7.1:

TABLE 1.7.1: INTERNAL VERSUS EXTERNAL SWOT

INTERNAL	EXTERNAL
STRENGTHS	OPPORTUNITIES
WEAKNESSES	THREATS

Using these headings, you can start to develop a much clearer picture of the components that make up the campaign. By identifying and knowing where you are in relation to each of these elements, you will be in a much stronger position to create a sustainable vision (at least for the duration of the campaign's 'live' stage).

These types of analysis will also help you identify the flaws in your plan; acknowledging these – at least within the team – allows you to seek balances and gain confidence in the plan and the campaign. This supports the crowd too in that they will now feel they are giving their consent to a well conceived and thought-out idea in which they can trust.

One of the simplest ways of completing a SWOT analysis is to use bullet points to highlight the various elements in each section. As an example, let us imagine a campaign is trying to refurbish a skate park and bring it up to date. We will presume the team has completed a STEEPLED analysis and answered all the relevant questions according to their needs. A SWOT may look something like this:

TABLE 1.7.2: SIMPLE ISSUES ADDRESSED IN SWOT

INTERNAL	EXTERNAL
STRENGTHS	OPPORTUNITIES
• Local councillor has backed the campaign	• Local sponsors agreed
WEAKNESSES	THREATS
• Lack of management experience	• Council elections soon (change?)

From the outset, your SWOT analysis will probably be a lot more complex than this simple example. These are typical issues that could be faced and are easily identified and lots more can, and should, be included in this analysis. Some may question why the councillor has been included in the 'internal strengths section. Surely she is an outsider?

Technically that is correct, but once her agreement to the cause (her consent) has been given she can now be categorized as internal, part of the core. Her involvement can be a huge strength as her support and lobbying of other councillors and the wider community to highlight the value of the campaign, can now start.

In her role as councillor, she has 'inside' knowledge of the workings of the local council which could be a tremendous help. She may be in a position to offer advice and help the campaign by identifying people to whom you should speak about growing support.

But of course, this could all change because, as we see in the threats section, local elections are coming and she may lose her seat on the council. She could still be an asset to the campaign in terms of her knowledge of the workings of the council, but her influence, if the council switches colours, could be lessened.

From a very simple example (just four bullet points) we are already starting to draw out some potential problems and issues that could impact the campaign. This demonstrates how useful this type of analysis is in helping to help clarify where different impacts may emerge, but how do you neutralize a negative impact?

PLANNING - TOWS ANALYSIS

A recognized method for doing this is to use a TOWS table that will balance strengths with weaknesses, and opportunities with threats and so on. TOWS is an acronym that uses the same letters as SWOT but with emphasis switching to a more balanced view of your campaign. In other words, it helps you see, and then neutralize, any negatives that have been identified in the SWOT analysis by matching them with positives.

The example below in table 1.7.3 demonstrates how each of the external factors (opportunities and threats) can be best matched with the internal factors (strengths and weaknesses).

TABLE 1.7.3: TOWS TABLE

TOWS TABLE	OPPORTUNITIES	THREATS
STRENGTHS	O-S	T-S
WEAKNESSES	O-W	T-W

Questions can now be asked about how best to maximize the positives and minimize the negatives. These could include:

O-S = How can we use our strengths to maximize this crowdfunding opportunity?
O-W = Can the opportunities be used to counter the weaknesses in the campaign?

T-S = Threats to the campaign are serious so what strengths can we use to counter these?

T-W = How do the threats and weaknesses match? How can we reduce these negatives?

All these questions are taken from the SWOT analysis already completed – there should be nothing new in TOWS that has not already been reported in the SWOT.

In a way, this is a counterbalancing method and it is fairly simple to understand and implement. This should be done at the pre-campaign stage as it will help to develop better strategies as layers of complexity are added to the campaign.

PLANNING – CRITICAL PATH

If you are building a house, you cannot plaster and paint the walls before they have been erected. There needs to be a sequence, an order, to the building of a house. Some things are essential at the beginning while others can wait until a little later. Some things will need to be done at the same time as other things.

Thinking through this sequence of what needs to be done and when is the base of the critical path approach. In essence, this method establishes the sequence of actions and needs in a project. Building a house, managing a theatre production or creating a crowdfunding campaign all comprise elements that need completing in sequence.

This is where the critical path technique can be really helpful. It demonstrates (visually) what needs to be completed before the next task can begin. It also shows the timings of these activities so a team knows where they are at any point in time, and what should be done before the next task is started.

Begin by listing all the things that need doing to create a campaign. These should be on your CPP and they can now be ordered to show what needs to be completed first, second, third and so on. Once this is done you have a list which can be ordered in the sequence needed, like this:

- Write vision and mission (1→1)
- Create story (1→1)
- Identify suppliers (2→3)
- Schedule filming (3→3)
- Photo shoot (3→5 / P - 4)
- Write storyboard (3→3)
- Profile targets (3→3 / P - 6)
- Establish tiers/promises (4→5 / P - 7)
- Assess communication channels (4→5)
- Audit platforms (5→5 / P - 11)
- Audit campaigns (5→5 / P - 10)
- Write scripts (5→5)
- Plan updates (6)
- Set post-campaign strategies (6)
- Finalize costs / timings (6 / P - 14)

In brackets after each activity is a number with an arrow to another number. This represents the week this activity starts and the week by which it must be completed. For example, activity 1 (write vision and mission) starts in week 1(1) and has to be completed/finished in week 1 (→1).

Activity 5 (photo shoot) starts in week 3 (3) and must be completed by week 5 (→5), so there is a two-week period within which this activity can be completed. But it is also a 'parallel' activity which is why it has (P - 4) in the sequence. This means the activity is one that can be done at the same time as another activity. This activity (photo shoot) can be done in parallel with activity 4 (schedule filming).

Likewise activity 7 (profile targets) can be done in parallel, or at the same time as, activity 6 (write storyboard). Activities that have no 'P' are what are known as *consecutive*; that is they can be done on their own and are not necessarily done at the same time as other activities. Activities 1 to 4 on the above example are all activities that can be done this way.

Once the list is complete it can be transferred to a spreadsheet or a table as shown in table 1.7.4:

TABLE 1.7.4: EXAMPLE CRITICAL PATH

	ACTIVITY	START→ END	P
1	WRITE VISION AND MISSION	1 → 1	
2	CREATE STORY	1 → 1	
3	IDENTIFY SUPPLIERS	2 → 3	
4	SCHEDULE FILMING	3 → 3	
5	PHOTO SHOOT	3 → 5	4
6	WRITE STORYBOARD	3 → 3	
7	PROFILE TARGETS	3 → 3	6
8	ESTABLISH TIERS/PROMISES	4 → 5	7
9	ASSESS COMMUNICATION CHANNELS	4 → 5	
10	AUDIT PLATFORMS	5 → 5	11
11	AUDIT CAMPAIGNS	5 → 5	10
12	WRITE SCRIPTS	5 → 5	
13	PLAN UPDATES	6	
14	SET POST-CAMPAIGN STRATEGIES	6	
15	FINALIZE COSTS / TIMINGS	6	14

For even greater effect, colour can be added and the weekly Start → End points could even be actual dates rather than broader weeks. The next stage is to transfer this data on to a table that can demonstrate just the start / end points - as demonstrated in table 1.7.5 below where the green cell means start and the red means end. Purely red cells have the same start/end week.

TABLE1.7.5: VISUAL DISPLAY OF ACTIVITIES AND THEIR START/ END TIMES

WEEK / ACTIVITY	1	2	3	4	5	6
1	■					
2	■					
3		▨	■			
4			■			
5			▨	▨	■	
6			■			
7			■			
8				▨	■	
9				▨	■	
10					■	
11					■	
12					■	
13						■
14						■
15						■

This may seem a long-winded way of setting out your activities and what needs to be done, but by going through this three-phase writing exercise (list, table and colour table) the activities may be refined and possibly re-ordered as the writing process continues. It can also help to get a team committed to a course of action as they have had direct input and worked on the schedule.

Finally, it can also be helpful to have a fresh pair of eyes look over your scheduling and make suggestions that may not have been seen by the author working in isolation.

PLANNING - SMART AIMS

To help everyone in a team to understand the overall objectives of a campaign there should be clearly articulated aims that will help reach the objective (the end point). The real difference between aims and objectives is set out later in section 2.5. This section is an introduction to the planning process and some of the tools that can help create a well-defined and executed plan. SMART is one of these tools and it is an acronym for:

- Specific
- Measurable
- Agreed
- Realistic
- Timely

A campaign's aims must be *specific* in that they are separated and clearly set out in a way that means they can be detailed and understood. This includes who is responsible for each task. Campaigns often encounter major problems because time has not been taken to set out the aims properly. Doing this early in the planning stages will mean the campaign should flow with much greater ease.

Aims should be *measurable* because progress has to be discernible in some way. Early in the planning stages, the measurement methods should also be clearly set out so everyone involved with the campaign knows what to look for and what they are using to keep tabs on the progress (or lack of progress) of the project.

Once again, clarity is the key in communicating this aspect to the team. There may also be more than one metric being calculated in a project at any time, so it is important that team members have a good understanding of the metrics they are expected to keep an eye on – and when.

Aims must be agreed by team members. This also helps members feel they have made a commitment to the project. Once this is made they rarely let the project down by refusing or withdrawing this commitment.

The aims should also be *realistic*; they should be sensible and rational because, if they are not, then they are less likely to be met and the whole project may be put in danger of failing. Unrealistic aims can really damage a team's morale, while aims that seem realistic are a wonderful motivator.

Finally, aims should be *timely* because the whole project must be deliverable within a workable time span, and for this to be achieved, the aims have to be met in good time. This is reflected in the critical path scheduling seen previously. Timeliness of the aims will mean the bigger objective(s) being met in good time and delivered according to the plan.

All the planning in the world cannot stop every minor hiccup from happening in a project. Things can, and often do, go wrong for all manner of reasons and this is to be expected in any project – especially one dealing with a crowd of people who are unknown to management.

With some kind of decent structure behind the plan, the likelihood is that any deviation will have much less negative impact on the campaign.

TASK 12: PLANNING

COMPLETE A STEEPLED ANALYSIS

COMPLETE A SWOT / TOWS ANALYSIS

COMPLETE A CRITICAL PATH

START YOUR PLANNING ON THE CPP

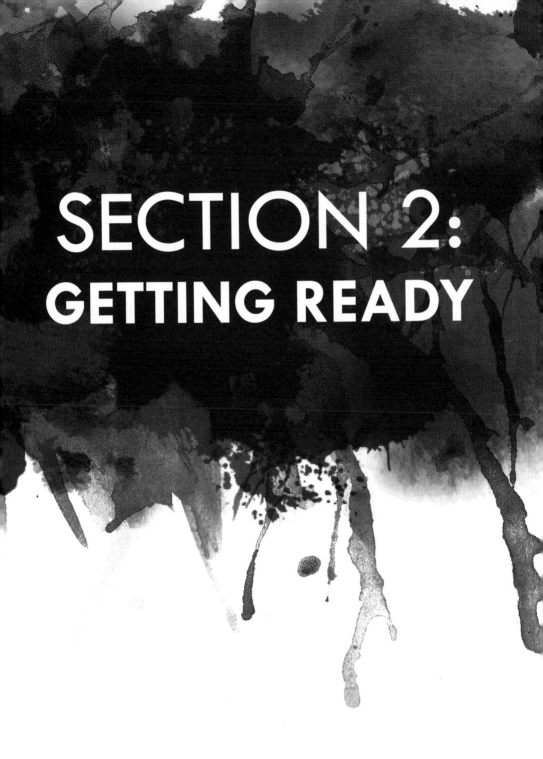

SECTION 2:
GETTING READY

CONTENTS

2.1

SCOPE

The scope of your project needs to be considered from two angles: the geographical connection of the project and the size of the intended impact. These may at first seem unimportant to your campaign. They may even seem separate and unconnected, but think about it for a moment; if you have no idea from where the people are coming who will support you and equally, if you have no idea what kind of impact this campaign is going to make, it is likely that the campaign will fail to reach its target.

If you are raising funds for a local music event, you are not likely to attract funds from a very broad network of people beyond those interested in the festival, your friends and your family. For this reason, the location's appeal and the support the event is offering to local music producers and fans, is much more concentrated. On the other hand, if this is a nationally significant event then, of course, your appeal through the campaign is going to be much wider and benefit a bigger demographic with the potential for a huge impact.

Therefore, when you address the scope of the project you need to think about the geographical appeal of the project and the impact it is likely to have. By knowing and recognizing the geographical appeal of the project, you can target the audience you are trying to reach with much more precision. This will also help marketing as it ensures that the message in the crowdfunding campaign matches the target demographic; in other words, making sure the people you want to be supporting you are able to understand the message in the campaign.

However, measuring the impact may be more problematic because it can be a negative or a positive thing depending on your point of view. A music festival, for example, can be an amazing chance to showcase some local talent, while for others it is an unnecessary hassle where the roads get blocked and the noise levels in the surrounding countryside become unbearable.

These issues need consideration in your crowdfunding campaign because it can be very bad news if people start complaining or posting negative comments about your campaign through social media channels. These effects can be deep and result in failure (or in extreme cases, the removal of the campaign from the platform). In the above example, imagine if you launch the campaign and then local residents start to complain via social media about your project. How would you handle this situation without appearing to be confrontational?

For the crowd, it would look like you have not done your homework properly and members might assume the project is not a very well thought-out idea. We encountered asymmetrical information earlier in section 1.4, and here again, we have a problem with this very issue. The crowd members think they know titbits about the team and the project; however nobody has all the information and some of these 'facts' will be based on speculation. This puts the crowd in a tricky position; members now rely on their peers to pass on information about the project. They must believe that the information they are receiving is of a high enough quality that they can trust it and make a decision based on it.

Do you think people would back a project they thought was not very well thought-through? No, they probably wouldn't. They would probably listen to their peers and make a decision based on the information collated from the updates and social media channels. Therefore, impact needs careful consideration on many levels, not least the economic, environmental, social and political ones.

One way of dealing with these issues is to think about the types of impact the campaign may have and the potential effects or consequences. A simple mapping exercise can help generate suggestions that may counter-balance the negative consequences. An example of this is given below in table 2.1.1. Here, we use the idea of the local music festival as an example. The potential negatives and positives are given along with a small amount of detail about the local people who might be affected the likely impact on them.

TABLE 2.1.1: IMPACT ASSESSMENT

AREA	NEGATIVE	POSITIVE
ECONOMIC	No sales in local shops during event as locals stay home	Broader impact of greater number visiting the area and spending in local facilities
ENVIRONMENTAL	Congestion on local roads at both beginning and end of festival	Traffic management plans to be introduced to enable smoother flow
SOCIAL	Local events postponed during festival. Normal social centres see reduced use	Local population will be given free access to event and reduced fees for stalls/stands
POLITICAL	Need for extra policing, traffic control and emergency services	Introduce clean-up operation for site. Sponsorship of local emergency services

It should be stressed that this is a very simple model and yours may be much more complex. The point is that the model can be used with all kinds of projects no matter how complex or simple they are and no matter how big or insurmountable the problem may first appear. It must also be stressed that you must be honest when doing an impact assessment. The crowd tends to be very good at detecting errors or outright false claims, so be clear and honest in your campaigning.

Transparency is king in crowdfunding. If something 'smells a bit fishy' it will soon be ousted by the crowd (look at the Mythic game on page 28). You cannot underestimate the ability of the crowd to detect and report issues of fairness or wrong-doing. That's not to say mistakes are not made, but most of the time the crowd will quite quickly pick up on things that don't add up. The golden rules are to be ethical and 100% honest – if the project is unethical or against your personal values, you should really be asking yourself why you need to be doing this.

Completing an impact assessment will not eliminate the negative impacts, but it will prepare you and your team with counter points of view to offer those who are not convinced your project should go ahead (or elements of the project need to be changed). Remember too, that there may be no need for an assessment of this nature. It may be that your project presents no negative impacts that need to be considered and managed.

TASK 13: IMPACT

WHAT IS THE GEOGRAPHICAL SCOPE OF THIS PROJECT?

THINK ABOUT AN IMPACT ASSESSMENT AUDIT FOR YOUR PROJECT – DO YOU NEED TO DO ONE?

IF YOU ANSWER NO, FINE. IF YOU ANSWER YES, NOW IS THE TIME TO START ONE.

WHAT WILL BE THE HEADINGS IN YOUR ASSESSMENT?

HOW WILL YOU FIND PROBLEMS AND SOLUTIONS?

2.2

RESEARCH

There are, without exception, there two related elements that are integral to the success of any raise. These are knowing what you are offering the funders and knowing what you are doing with the business model post-campaign (see section 5). These are not always easy or obvious to ascertain and, on the following pages, you will learn a little about the approaches that have worked best for campaigns we have been involved with in the past. However, this is a general view and you may need to adjust any models demonstrated here to suit your particular campaign.

Every crowdfunding campaign is seeking one thing: the crowd's consent to create a vision. As mentioned earlier, we call this crowdconsent, a made-up word that nevertheless encapsulates the essence of what is being attempted through the endeavour. The consent that you are seeking must be focused on the campaign.

A campaign that is seeking consent to create a general vision (a museum, for example) will find it much trickier than a campaign seeking consent to preserve a particular artefact or acquire a specific something for the museum. This is because the specific item is much more focused, there is no uncertainty about what the campaign is trying to achieve - it is transparent.

When researching your campaign's target funders, start by breaking down the types of funder you want to attract. Remember that by knowing exactly what you want to achieve through the campaign, this will be much easier for you to manage.

The problem for most campaigns is that there are many categories of funder. Not only this, but they are influenced by other funders who may not even be your main target of the campaign. Even more complex is a situation where the main target (and possibly the outer targets of the campaign) are themselves influenced by another party altogether. As you can imagine, this situation can become quite difficult to manage properly as is demonstrated in figure 2.2.1:

FIGURE 2.2.1: THE COMPLEXITY OF INFLUENCERS

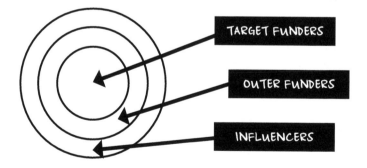

In figure 2.2.1, you can see the target funders are in the centre while there are still significant 'outer funders' who also need to be considered as they will be adding value to the project too. But on top of this, there is also a category of 'influencers' who are not even adding value directly to the campaign.

Despite this, their influence is necessary to help nudge the outer and target funders into action. So this project still needs to identify, and then communicate with, this group for the campaign to be successful.

This situation is not that uncommon and an example would be the skate park mentioned in the introduction. Target funders could be the parents of the teenagers who will be using the park. The outer funders could be the wider community that need engagement to be convinced of the benefits offered by the park, in order for the raise to succeed. Influencers of these inner groups could be local political activists, club leaders (bowling, history, parents with young children) and, of course, local media.

Once these are identified, the real work can begin as you start to assess their needs and how this project will benefit them. One way to do this is to ask, "what's in it for them?" with each of the groups. By answering this simple question, you can quite quickly start to build a better picture of the drivers that will motivate them into action.

Problems can still arise in this approach if you make too many assumptions based on 'bad' evidence. For example, interviewing people is fine but are you sure they are the people to whom you should be talking?

It may be that you are interviewing the wrong people or interviewing in the wrong place or at the wrong time. Asking questions about public transport is fine, but if you ask car drivers, you will get a very different response from those who use buses or bicycles. You may not need to interview all these people but by interviewing a good cross-section you will be able to build a much more accurate picture of the crowd's perspective.

In some circumstances, it may emerge from this research that the aims of the campaign need to be adjusted or changed to match the aims of the crowd more closely. It could be that you have identified one set of values that you thought was held by the crowd but, through the research, you find that members actually want or need something different. This is not a bad thing; in fact it is a very good thing, as you now know exactly what the crowd desires and how you can satisfy this desire through your campaign.

The key is to be sure you know who you are going to ask, when and why. By knowing this, it will quite quickly become clear that the action you are seeking from the target funders will be much easier to obtain.

You will know who they are and their preferences and, with this in mind, you will be able to create a campaign that 'speaks' to the target funders. When you speak to them, what you are really trying to do is to develop a story that the crowd finds sufficiently riveting to inspire it to take action. In other words, once they approve of the story and the vision your campaign is creating they are more likely to act, they are more likely to give you their consent.

This 'story' is called a narrative and the approval you are seeking , crowdconsent. With these two things in the bag you are much more likely to enjoy a successful outcome. But to align the narrative and gain crowdconsent you still need to find out who it is you should be targeting in the first place. In the past, marketers referred to segmentation of the population and all this really meant was classifying people according to certain criteria such as their income level.

This is fine and it works quite well when you have a product to launch or a service you wish to start up (and either might be your case). Segmentation can offer a powerful overview of the target funders for your campaign and it allows you the freedom to create the segments at will. In effect, you have control over the creation of these segments and who does/does not belong in them.

This needs careful consideration.

For example, you can segment all skate park users into one category based on their age, or all car drivers based on the distance they travel to work. The problem lies in the very creation of these categories; they are artificial collections of statistical (quantitative) information. They fail to tell you anything about the character of the people who are categorized in the segments you create.

At minivation, we have found that, rather than identifying a group of people based on an abstract definition that we have created, it is more helpful to identify segments that already exist, people who have formed their own category, spontaneously, who have already come together to create a community around something or some issue. This has been called 'tribal consumerism' and it is attracting a lot of attention in the marketing world.

This is special because the tribe (the people who make up the segment) come together to create some form of value often without the incentive of a brand. Their focus may be on a branded product or service, but the point is, the brand did not instigate this activity. The tribe is also free to switch between brands, which is worrying for brand management.

Tribes can also be 'for profit' or 'not-for-profit' which can present a problem for traditional brands. Another unique feature is that tribes identify with one another collectively, they share experiences, feelings and emotions, which can reinforce identity and its members can engage together and create action in response to a situation. This is where the real difference between traditional market segmentation lies. With the more traditional approach of segmentation, the group members were together because you, the researcher, grouped people together. But with the tribal approach, people are grouped together because they chose to belong to this socially-constructed group.

Therefore, they can persuade one another more easily to act in a certain way, for example, giving their consent.

With segmentation, this type of action was almost impossible as the group was constructed out of thin air by a researcher. There was no social cohesion (or glue) binding members together. A tribe, on the other hand, is a grouping that may have occurred because of the cohesion the tribe offers. There is a social element to the formation of the tribe and the tribe members' willingness to interact with one another about the central issue.

A good example of this would be the Satellite Applications Catapult Didcot Group. This group was advertising through the UK version of Meet Up, a site dedicated to helping people find others with a similar interest to their own.

They could then meet in real time to build, collaborate, discuss or make things. This group were organizing a hackathon. For a better flavour, read the passage below taken straight from their Meet-Up page:

"Satellite Applications Catapult will be a base for space related hackathons at the newly refurbished HQ in Didcot. We will be hosting events lasting 2 days, in which a large number of people meet to engage in collaborative computer programming: This 48-hour hackathon is to build new web and mobile services revolving around satellite data. Solutions can range from predicting natural disasters, Climate change, anything you can think of to tantalize the judges, using a wealth of satellite data. Catapult are activity looking for great ideas to support! All Our Event will be free, we will have great free food, Place to sleep, shuttle bus. Were not just looking for programmers, Entrepreneurs, people with ideas, mathematicians, everyone is welcome. And we are looking for a diverse group of people to get a full range of ideas, Sign up and take part in hacking space data." [sic] 26

Although the focus of the meeting is very specific, the call to get involved goes out to a very wide range of people. This is a classic tribe coming together for a very specific reason in an equally specific timeframe.

Imagine the traditional marketers trying to identify all the segments within this group, it would be a very difficult task. But when these people are seen as a 'tribe' the detail of exactly how much each member earns or the type of car they drive becomes much less important. More important is the means of support to this group that a campaign could offer.

This is the key in tribal investigations – the support that can be provided through the activity of the campaign or the resultant vision that is being created. Think of it this way: in the past, organizations would create something to be delivered to an identified consumer.

This changes with tribalism because the organization is now seeking ways of supporting the tribe's existence and help members with their communications and identity; not through domination of these aspects but by being much more open and taking on board what the tribe has to say.

For your campaign, this is really rich information that could help you blend together your thinking with that of the tribe. This could (and should) create something that the tribe really wants to support.

Thinking about the campaign overall, once you know what you are looking for, the question really becomes where do you look for this information.

A really useful way to think about this is to break down your search into three distinct areas:
• Researching tribes
• Auditing other campaigns
• Auditing your own campaign

We will look at these three elements in turn below.

RESEARCHING TRIBES

Finding the tribe to research is not an easy task because they can be formed very quickly around an issue and then they can evaporate into thin air just as quickly. So having a finger on the pulse of what is happening in your sector is vital.

There are many areas that can be scanned regularly for information and indications that tribal activity is taking place. These can be in some fairly obvious places but equally in some really obscure ones. Table 2.2.1 provides some places to look and the scope of tribal activity.

TABLE 2.2.1: WHERE TO LOCATE A TRIBE AND THEIR SCOPE

FIND THROUGH	LOCAL	NATIONAL	INTERNATIONAL
ONLINE SEARCH	X	X	X
SOCIAL MEDIA	X	X	X
NATIONAL PRESS	X	X	X
EVENTS/EXHIBITIONS	X	X	X
NETWORKING	X	X	
CLUBS	X	X	
WORD OF MOUTH	X	X	
COMMUNITY BOARDS	X		
TOWN HALL	X		
TOURIST INFORMATION	X		
SHOP WINDOWS	X		

This is not an exhaustive list. But by creating your own list along these lines you will be able to identify tribes operating in your sector and with relevance to your campaign.

TIES

In 1973, a US university student, Mark Granovetter, published a paper that is still as significant today as it was then. His paper was titled *The Strength of Weak Ties.*[27]

It was significant because it showed how a population's network can affect outcomes for individuals and also whole groups.

In figure 2.2.1, we saw how influence can come from outside the target group from which we are seeking crowdconsent. This same influence is what Granovetter had been looking at back in 1973. His study went much deeper than our interest in how to crowdfund a project and was concerned with connections between group members and their motivations.

So what do we mean by strong or weak ties? The essence of these terms lies in the people with whom we associate and their ability to influence our actions. This is a simplistic view of these terms but it serves sufficiently for our purposes here as we deal with the live stage of a campaign.

Why this 1973 paper is so significant for us today is that Mr Granovetter (now Professor) found that the weak ties were often more likely to provide access to infrastructures and opportunities than were the strong ties. This may seem a little counter-intuitive, as the old saying goes, "It's not what you know, it's who you know". According to Granovetter this is correct, but the 'who' is more important once a little distance exists between you.

Those friends of friends you have heard lots about, who work for a local company for which you also would like to work can help you get a foot in the door. It has proven similar in crowdfunding. Figure 2.2.1 looked at the influencers that any campaign management may need to consider for their campaign to succeed. It is often the case (though, of course, there are always exceptions) that these influencers are in the 'weak tie' grouping rather than the 'strong tie' grouping.

The message I am trying to get across is that the weaker ties in your network are often the ones to whom you need to reach out. So when planning your campaign and thinking about the live stages, a primary concern should be how to reach these weaker ties.

Your research should have provided a good overview of these ties as well as the tribes (see p117) that must be reached for your campaign to succeed. There should by now also be a sound framework for the types of communication and the channels that will be used to distribute the campaigns message.

There is another consideration for campaign management: the tertiary ties. These are a much more modern take on the original research conducted by Granovetter. In crowdfunding, we often experience a third set of ties who can greatly enhance the success of a campaign.

This third set of ties (tertiary ties) is even further removed from the first two sets. The individuals in this category pick up on messages being broadcast through social media channels and the crowdfunding platforms themselves. They may be connected in some way to the strong/weak ties network but not in the same sense that the strong ties are connected to the weak ties. This link is much more tenuous than the strong/weak link and tertiary ties may even be unconnected with either tie within the inner parameters. Another point is that the tertiary tie group only exists in bits - the atoms rarely actually meet.

Below is a model that attempts to help visualize these connections:

FIGURE 4.1: TERTIARY, STRONG AND WEAK TIE MODEL

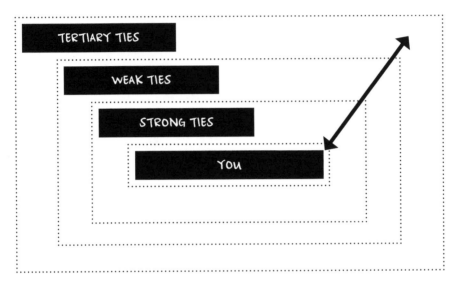

There are some very broad statistics about how much funding comes from strong ties (estimates range between 0% and 40% depending on the model) and how much this impacts the quality signal that gets passed on to the weaker and then tertiary ties in the campaign.[28] At this stage, you are live and so all these plans must now be put into motion and the ties brought up to date with the campaign's activities.

All the planning that went before this 'live' stage now needs to be implemented and this means the real work begins. The first thing is to get networking like crazy. Spread the knowledge that the campaign has gone live and remind those in your strong, weak and tertiary ties of the promises they made to you about giving their consent or, at the very least, spreading the word. If you pre-crowdfunded then, of course, you have an advantage because you will have spread the word and activated your network's attention, they should be poised for action.

AUDITING OTHER CAMPAIGNS

An audit simply means an inspection of something. When launching something new into the market, even a new unseen product or service, organizations always look for competition and look closely at what this competition offers.

If they are launching a new widget that has never been seen before they will look at what customers are using currently. Once they know, they look at the organizations satisfying this need. They often treat these organizations as competitors.

Thinking this way in your campaign is vital.

The difference, of course, is that you are seeking to understand the other campaigns you can find that are close to what you are doing. Categories on the various platforms are good for this and can help you quickly identify campaigns in the same sector as yours.

Be careful about replication where a campaign is listed on a platform more than once – some platforms are well known for this as it helps them increase the statistical number of campaigns they have in each category which can make them look much more active than they are. There are legitimate reasons for doing this, but it does mean that you will need to look at several categories to find listings that may be similar to yours.

Keep a record of your findings that includes all the most important information; an example is given on the next page:

TABLE 2.2.2: RECORDING COMPETITOR CAMPAIGN INFORMATION

PLATFORM	NAME	RAISE	TIME	NOTES
THE PLATFORM THE CAMPAIGN IS WITH	NAME OF THE CAMPAIGN OR TITLE	HOW MUCH THEY ARE SEEKING	HOW LONG THE CAMPAIGN IS RUNNING FOR AND WHEN (SEASON)	ADDITIONAL INFORMATION

There may be other relevant information that you need to include in your search. This is just an idea for a template to get you started. Try to make checking this a routine activity so that you have the most up-to-date information to support judgments and to bear in mind while you think through your strategy. The more campaigns you analyze in this manner, the more familiar you will become with what works on particular platforms.

Also bear in mind that the timing of the campaign could be important. This could be the season in which the campaign either runs or launches. It could even be an actual date that is significant to the campaign in some way.

For example, a product like a skateboard might be better launched to coincide with a traditional gift-giving season (like Christmas) but a new sun lounger might be better launched for the drier, warmer seasons. Something connected to prostate cancer might be worth promoting in November when the international Movember fundraising activity happens.[29]

Seasonality, or a specific date dedicated to a given topic, can help your campaign by association. A campaign does not need ownership of the season or the date, but a strong association could be a big advantage in attracting an audience. So, when auditing other campaigns, taking this element into consideration can help as it provides a little more of the overall picture.

AUDITING YOUR CAMPAIGN

An audit of your own campaign provides you with an overview of the project and tells you where the strengths and weaknesses are. This will provide you with confidence and also the chance to reflect on where you are right now and where you would like to be in the near future. Thinking this through at this stage will help you to balance the weaknesses of the campaign with the strengths (see SWOT analysis in section 1.7, p95).

It is also a great opportunity for you to familiarize yourself with the details of the campaign that may have been neglected while you were considering the bigger picture and searching through the competitor's campaigns. It may be the chance to breathe and take stock of things as you set out on paper all the various elements that contribute to your campaign.

When working in a team on a project, it is useful to get each member to audit the campaign separately and then compare insights. It can be very surprising when the team members see the campaign from other perspectives (even when you have been working closely together).

If time will not allow this exercise, then audit various sections of the campaign (see the CPP in section 1.6, p82) and then compare the sections together. The key to either exercise is to be open to the interpretation of others.

An audit of your campaign is a chance for you to reflect and assess your campaign's likely success. Be honest about its weaknesses as you do this and answer the following questions:

- Who are the targets of this campaign?
- Do we understand the benefits we offer these target groups?
- Have we identified the relevant tribes?

- Do we understand the motivations behind their tribalism?
- Do we understand what's in it for them when they might give their consent?
- Have we identified the influencers of these tribes?

At this stage, you should have good answers to these questions and have a deeper understanding not just of why the questions are being asked but of how they are relevant to your specific campaign.

TASK 14: RESEARCH AUDIT

PLAN OUT YOUR RESEARCH (WHERE WILL YOU LOOK, WHEN, HOW?) AND THEN CONDUCT YOUR AUDITS.

RESEARCH SUMMARY

It is essential to consider that there may be more than one group of funders with which you need to communicate in your campaign. These groups may themselves be influenced by outer groups which may not even be in a position (or desire) to fund your campaign; nevertheless these groups may influence your targets and so you may need to ensure they are aware of, and supporting, your campaign.

These groups would traditionally have been categorized in artificially-constructed groups that would have enabled the targeted marketing of products to the group in question, but we suggest you adopt a 'tribal approach' whereby the groups are formed more organically around a topic and are helped by the campaign to sustain their existence. Tribal groups can take group action and make group decisions. These decisions can result (or not) in the tribe supporting your campaign – a form of consent that we call crowdconsent.

Audits are a smart way of acquiring information about the competition and about your own campaign. Through an audit, you can start to link your campaign, with much greater accuracy, to the motivation of the crowd.

2.3

PROMISES

Promises are important because a promise gives us confidence that something will happen in the future, an assurance will be honoured. But of course promises come in many different forms and with many different meanings.

"I promise to marry you" is very different to "I promise to help you move house". One is a long-term commitment to fulfil an obligation and the other is a short-term, one-off situation. Although it could be argued that both may involve physical and mental stress!

In crowdfunding, we use promises to make a commitment to the crowd as an assurance that we will add or create some future value. There are three components that make up a promise in crowdfunding as shown in figure 2.3.1:

FIGURE 2.3.1: THE PROMISE PROCESS

I. MATCH   >   II. PROMISE   >   III. DELIVER

MATCH

The first part of the process is to ensure your promises are a good match with the crowd. For example, you may decide to offer a T-shirt with a campaign message or logo on the front as a reward. But if you are aiming at a crowd whose members rarely or never wear T-shirts this reward is not a very good match.

Likewise, to 3D-print a fantasy character with the head of the funder as a reward is fine if the character is understood and liked by the crowd. But if the crowd does not understand the context of what you are offering or the fantasy figure is a random offering that has no connection with the campaign, then once again the match is not a good one.

Matching is just as it sounds: matching the promises the campaign makes with the crowd it is aiming at. This may seem obvious, but a quick look through some of the campaigns out there will show you that rewards are often not properly thought through by management. Really, this comes back to sound research.

PROMISE

As well as being a good match, the promise must also be desired or needed. Try to make it something practical that can be useful to the funder. However, the promise itself does not necessarily need to promote the campaign. If you go to a trade show you get free pens, coffee mugs, brochures and so on. These all serve to promote the company, product or service attending the show, but your promises are not necessarily serving this same function. The campaign (in most situations) is over and the crowd members are receiving their promise after the campaign has run, so as well as helping to promote the campaign, the promise is designed to be an inducement to encourage crowdconsent and enable you to achieve your vision.

It may, of course, promote the organization or team behind the campaign – but often this is not the primary reason the promise exists.

DELIVER

This is the physical delivery of promises in either electronic (bit) or physical (atom) form. No matter which, you will need to account for these when you are formulating your plans.

Delivery timings also need consideration. If you are delivering atoms, then you need to be sure the courier or postal service you use is reliable and costs have been calculated properly.

Making promises that are delivered as bits may seem like a cost-effective method, but remember these also need to be managed like physical goods. You need to ensure the email addresses for delivery are correct, for example. A simple means of doing this is to state, on the campaign's page, that you will deliver to the address funders provide – this shifts the emphasis to the funder to ensure they give correct details.

Another way of delivering bits is to set up something that can be downloaded by crowd members. For example, if you promise a downloadable version of a play you are crowdfunding, this needs to be organized and costs taken into account when you set out the budget for the campaign.

Likewise, printing off things using new technology such as a 3D printer takes time, materials and delivery methods, all of which need to be taken into account when you plan the campaign.

These options are all possible as long as they are planned properly and thought through before the campaign goes live.

TYPES OF PROMISE

Promises in crowdfunding can be a combination, or one of the following:

a) The promise to create the vision to a standard and within a time frame you set

b) The thank you you're offering

Both of these types of promise are pretty straightforward to understand, but getting the content of the promise right can be more problematic. This relies on there being a good match with the crowd's perceptions of the vision being created and the reality of that creation.

Each of the DREIM models has a unique promise that is being offered to the crowd and it is really important that the campaign management team plans its promise(s) thoroughly before moving to the live phase. Taking time early in the planning phase to consider this element can make a huge difference later when the campaign is live.

At minivation, we break down promises into two categories: primary and secondary. Primary promises are the first-level promises and are generally the reason why the crowd gives consent. The secondary promises could be thought of as a little extra value for the crowd for helping you along your way.

Each of the model's primary and secondary promises are set out below:

TABLE 2.3.1: CROWDFUNDING MODELS AND THEIR RESPECTIVE PROMISES

MODEL	PRIMARY PROMISE	SECONDARY PROMISE
DONATION	ACHIEVE A GOAL	WARM GLOW
REWARD	DELIVER A VALUE	SOCIAL CAPITAL
EQUITY	SHARE OF VENTURE	A GIFT
INTEREST	INTEREST	PAYBACK WITH NO DEFAULT AND ON TIME
MIXED	COMBINATION OF ABOVE	COMBINATION OF ABOVE

The promise for the donation model is normally a philanthropic act and so the main thing funders will want achieved is a goal of some description (for example, cycling from Land's End to John O' Groats) which will result in monies being raised for a social cause. Secondary promises here are the warm glow or feeling of doing something right for the cause in question.

The promise for the reward model starts to get a little more complicated as there is, as the name suggests, a reward for contributing to the campaign. Primary promises here tend to be either atoms or bits that are often custom-designed for the funder (or the category of funder). For the funder, a secondary promise could be in the form of social capital where bragging rights are given to the funder for being first to back a campaign and getting the personalized product. It should also be noted that the bigger the campaign grows, the greater the degree of social capital a funder can expect. This is important as it may help your planning for this scenario.[30]

In the equity model, the share of the venture is the primary promise but quite often campaign managers also throw in a little "thank you" with something extra (for example, a key ring or a memory stick) but these are discretionary, not compulsory. Once again, they need to be accounted for when the campaign is planned as there may be a cost in both providing them and delivering them.

In the interest model, payback of the original capital invested, plus a little interest, is the primary promise. Secondary to this is the notion of being paid back all the money in the transaction, and on time.

Each of these categories of promise can change slightly and this is why we have used the term 'normally' when setting out these promises. Each campaign is different and the need to be flexible when planning these promises is essential.

TASK 15: PROMISE

WORK OUT THE PROMISES YOUR CAMPAIGN WILL OFFER.

BUDGETING

No matter which DREIM model you decide is best for your campaign you will need to know the budget you have for achieving this goal and the costs you will incur in the process.

Promises must have a margin built in to them, and this includes the delivery of atoms to the crowd. In other words, the things that you offer as rewards or gifts must be bought or produced and then delivered while still making a profit for the campaign.

Let's imagine that a reward costs £5 to produce and deliver. This reward now has to be offered at a funding level greater than £5. If you offer it for £5 - the campaign makes nothing. If you offer it for £6, the campaign makes £1 so now the campaign is making a (small) profit on the reward. Obviously, the greater the amount over £5, the greater the profit; if the reward can be offered for £20, that's £15 towards the campaign – great!

Rewards can be fairly straightforward, like the example earlier of an equity raise that offered a keying as an extra little thank you. Rewards can also be very elaborate, and more often than not, give something of the product away – like a new app or drinking glass.

The more creative you can be the better, especially in the rewards model of crowdfunding. As an example, one of the best rewards we helped to create was a pre-recorded walk-on part in a live play. The lines for the character were written and the funder was filmed before the live event and then shown on screen as part of the play. It was a great reward because:

- It engaged the funder and their network
- It provided social capital for the funder
- There could have been more than one of these rewards
- The funder could have created their own lines
- Production costs were minimal

It was filmed on a cheap hand-held camera by the play's producer who knew enough about filming to make it look good. But the effect of this reward was brilliant as it gave the crowd a chance to actually be in the play and support it in a very special way.

It must be remembered that a reward has to be perceived to be fair. If you offer a reward that the crowds think is unfair or offer a reward for, a much too high a funding level, it is unlikely to receive very much attention. This is tricky and needs careful consideration before you make a final decision. To get this right, it must be included in the research you do for the campaign.

The different levels of reward offered are called tiers and they also have to be 'priced' right. If one tier is available for £5 then you cannot ask £20 for two (you should ask for £10 or under) and so on. This is an obvious mistake and it should be picked up by the platform before you go live.

As an example of how this could work, let us imagine your campaign is to enable the creation of a new range of differently shaped and coloured umbrellas that collect, filter and bottle rain water for the carrier to drink. You decide to call this product the 'umbottler'. You also decide to use reward as your crowdfunding model.
Therefore the umbottler is composed of four elements:

- The umbottler (the main component)
- The bottle (that collects the water)

- The filter (that extracts all the nasty things so a person can drink the water safely)
- A carry bag (keeps everything neat and tidy)

For now, let us also imagine you have got the costs of the product's manufacturing, shipping and all expenses worked out and you are happy that each unit will cost you £1.50 to produce and have ready either to sell or give away.

You have also identified the platform and have been in touch with its management team – it is excited about the product and has offered you some guidance on the length of time the campaign should run and you have also started networking-like-crazy to raise awareness of the upcoming campaign and also for the product more broadly.

After extensive research into crowdfunding (following the guidelines in section 2.2) and speaking with the platform management, you and your team decide on eight tiers of reward as follows:

TABLE 2.3.2: EXAMPLE OF REWARD TIERS

TIER	REWARD	PRICE (£)
1	A THANK YOU FROM THE TEAM	1
2	THANKS + UMBOTTLER	5
3	THANKS + UMBOTTLER + CARRY BAG	10
4	UMBOTTLER + BAG + 1 EXTRA FILTER	15
5	2 UMBOTTLERS + CARRY BAGS	20
6	2 UMBOTTLERS + 2 EVERYTHING (BAG, FILTER & BOTTLE)	40
7	3 UMBOTTLERS + BAGS	50
8	3 UMBOTTLERS + 3 EVERYTHING (BAG, FILTER & BOTTLE)	60

Now you have the reward tiers (eight of them), the reward details (what you are offering) and what the crowd will be asked to contribute to get this reward (the price).

You have checked that the rewards are aligned with one another; that the price reflected in the value is not too high or too little.

You have also conducted some primary research, pre-crowdfunded for deeper feedback and analysis, taken notice of this feedback and refined the campaign and table 2.3.2 is the result.

For external purposes this is excellent. But for internal purposes there is one thing missing: the margin the campaign will make in each tier.

This is straightforward to work out and can be a really great way to envisage how the tiers can affect the campaign. In the example in table 2.3.3 we will assume the following to produce, stock and deliver each unit:

- Each umbottler costs £1.50
- Each extra bottle costs £1
- Each extra filter costs £1
- Each carry bag costs £1

To calculate this we use the equation; price minus cost equals margin (price - cost = margin).

TABLE 2.3.3: EXAMPLE OF REWARD TIERS WITH COST AND MARGIN.

TIER	REWARD	PRICE (£)	COST	MARGIN
1	A THANK YOU FROM THE TEAM	1	0	1
2	THANKS + UMBOTTLER	5	1.5	3.5
3	THANKS + UMBOTTLER + CARRY BAG	10	2.5	7.5
4	UMBOTTLER + BAG + 1 EXTRA FILTER	15	3.5	11.5
5	2 UMBOTTLERS + CARRY BAGS	20	5	15
7	3 UMBOTTLERS + BAGS	30	7.5	22.5
6	2 UMBOTTLERS + 2 EVERYTHING (BAG, FILTER & BOTTLE)	40	9	31
8	3 UMBOTTLERS + 3 EVERYTHING (BAG, FILTER & BOTTLE)	60	13.5	46.5

From the crowd's perspective this looks fair as each tier is a simple calculation of the number of units being offered. It is a simple structure and one that is very easy to understand and follow – even if the crowd is not made up of mathematicians, people can easily work this out.

If you wanted to get a little more sophisticated, you could discount for larger amounts of product, but you need to check and recheck that you are still making enough of a margin to make it worthwhile and that the crowd can relate to the discount being offered. If the crowd members do not want or need a discount, then there is no point offering one.

When working out the costs of the campaign everything needs to be calculated to ensure that the campaign will not make a loss. The whole reason for the campaign is to generate a value of some description.

This means you and your team have a responsibility to ensure that the promises that are made through the campaign can be kept and delivered within the timeframes given and make enough money to enable the vision to be created.

So your responsibility is to check there is sufficient funding generated from the campaign to create the vision and that the promises can be delivered on time and to the quality specified. If you fail in these aspects there can be a dramatic and sudden backlash against you and the team.

Overall, the campaign will have certain intrinsic costs that need to be considered, these are:

- The production or creation of rewards
- The delivery of rewards
- Promotional materials
- Any travel costs
- The charges of the platform and the payment provider
- Any taxes for which the campaign may be liable
- Labour costs for staff members on the campaign

This is a generic overview of costs and there will be more than we have listed here that your campaign will need to consider before going live. If in doubt about this area, contact a local business help service provider (your local council should be able to help).[31]

Alternatively, speak to an accountant. Generally, they offer superb advice and are in many respects an underutilized resource by campaign management.

TASK 16: FULL REWARD COSTING

WORK OUT YOUR BUDGET

WORK OUT YOUR REWARDS COSTS

WORK OUT THE MARGINS FOR THESE REWARDS

FINALLY DO A FULL COSTING FOR THE CAMPAIGN REWARDS

2.4

TEAM

We now leave the rewards and start to look at the team dynamics of a crowdfunding campaign.

This is because teams are one of the most important elements of any campaign. This is especially true in equity or interest crowdfunding models as these generally have more traditional, businesslike visions with more traditional business models. It follows, therefore, that the audience will generally be more interested in those areas with models they can readily understand.

But no matter what the crowdfunding model, when you list team members, it is important to tell the crowd not just who they are but also a little about their background. Their experience is what really counts here, and next to experience, who they know.

Teams that have a successful track record and have been performing over a longer period of time are the optimal type. Reasons for this vary, but generally, the teams that have a track record offer steadiness in what may be a turbulent first few months (or years) post-campaign.

This is critical for campaigns that are launching a new product or service in a commercial market. For the creative industries, it may be less of a priority for the crowd as they are often looking to back a one-off project that is not going to grow any further. But even in the creative sector, the power of the team and the experience and social network they can bring to the project, can have a dramatic effect.

It should also be noted that although a team member may know a prominent figure in society (for example a VIP) – they may not want (or be in a position to able to) approach this person for the purpose of the campaign.

This can be quite difficult if the person feels pressured or bullied into having to badger this contact, on the basis that the campaign will fail if they do not. This would not be acceptable behaviour for the management of any ethical campaign.

A team member may suggest they are in a position to help in this way – this should be welcomed as a positive contribution to the campaign, but in no way should any team member feel they are being forced to use their personal or professional contacts. If they do feel this, the morale of the team will start to falter quite quickly and this can have some nasty results for any campaign.

At minivation, we often use a series of mini-audits to record who is who in the team (see table 2.4.1). This can also help with more complex campaigns when the teams may be lots of sole traders and freelancers who are coming together to help one project before being dispersed to work on a completely different project.

With this type of team, it is very handy to start recording who they know and who they may be able to call on to help promote, or even fund, the campaign.

TABLE 2.4.1: TEAM MEMBER BASIC INFORMATION

NAME:
THEIR TRACK RECORD:
WHO THEY KNOW:
WHO CAN THEY CALL ON?
OTHER RELEVANT EXPERIENCE?
BIO IN 400 WORDS:

This is a great way to record basic information about each team member and get them to complete the biography of themselves in 400 words (or fewer). With their permission, this information can now be used in the main pages of the campaign to inform the crowd about the team, a kind of introduction to each team member.

It may be that the project's founder has a social network of 300 people which would be a nice starting point. But if we start to look at team members and the number of people to whom they are connected, this number of 300 may be multiplied several times.

Not all these connections will promote or contribute to the campaign of course, but by maximizing the number of people to which the campaign can be exposed, you are increasing the likelihood of at least some of these people adding to the campaign in some form. In general, we tend to work on the basis that 10% of any social media channels will possibly interact with the campaign.

So if the team can produce a combination of 5,000 connections (that is through all channels added together) you should work on the likelihood that 500 are more likely to engage with the campaign rather than the total number of 5,000.

This is worked like this:
$5,000 \div 100 = 50$ (this is the start of working out the percentage points)

Then taking the 50 above, multiply it by the percentage points (in this case 10) you want to work out and this gives you the final figure:
$50 \times 10 = 500$

One way to start a mini-audit for this is simply to ask team members to tell you their numbers in their social networks. If they are reluctant to give you this information then you could ask for a scaled idea of the number, as shown in table 2.4.2 on the following page:

TABLE 2.4.2: GETTING A FEEL FOR THE NUMBERS IN A TEAM'S SOCIAL NETWORK

IN ORDER FOR THE CAMPAIGN TO PLAN ITS IMPACT WE WOULD LIKE TO ASK YOU TO CIRCLE BELOW THE APPROXIMATE NUMBER OF PEOPLE ENGAGED WITH YOUR SOCIAL NETWORKS.

PLEASE SPECIFY ANY OTHER CHANNELS IN THE BLANK SPACES PROVIDED.

NAME:

CHANNEL	NUMBER					PROFESSIONAL NETWORK?	
FACEBOOK	0-50	51-100	101-300	301-500	500+	YES	NO
TWITTER	0-50	51-100	101-300	301-500	500+	YES	NO
BLOGS	0-50	51-100	101-300	301-500	500+	YES	NO
	0-50	51-100	101-300	301-500	500+	YES	NO
	0-50	51-100	101-300	301-500	500+	YES	NO
	0-50	51-100	101-300	301-500	500+	YES	NO
	0-50	51-100	101-300	301-500	500+	YES	NO
	0-50	51-100	101-300	301-500	500+	YES	NO
	0-50	51-100	101-300	301-500	500+	YES	NO
	0-50	51-100	101-300	301-500	500+	YES	NO

Team members may feel a bit awkward or embarrassed about giving away this kind of information, so check first that they are happy to give you an accurate number or at least an indication of the number. If they are happy to provide accurate numbers use table 2.4.3 and if not, then use table 2.4.2. Most team members are happy to provide accurate information – especially once they realize the purpose of providing this information and what can be contributed through providing it. Transparency is a key component in crowdfunding and this applies just as much internally with the team and management of the campaign as it does externally with the crowd.

TABLE 2.4.3: GETTING A MORE ACCURATE FEEL FOR THE NUMBERS IN A TEAM'S SOCIAL NETWORK

IN ORDER FOR THE CAMPAIGN TO PLAN ITS IMPACT WE WOULD LIKE TO ASK YOU TO INDICATE BELOW, THE APPROXIMATE NUMBER OF PEOPLE ENGAGED WITH YOUR SOCIAL NETWORKS. PLEASE SPECIFY ANY OTHER CHANNELS IN THE BLANK SPACES PROVIDED.		
NAME:		
CHANNEL	NUMBER	PROFESSIONAL NETWORK?
FACEBOOK		YES NO
TWITTER		YES NO
BLOGS		YES NO
		YES NO
		YES NO
		YES NO

In no way should team members be forced or pushed to give you this information – it should be volunteered. If they do feel pressured, or if you are asking them to reveal sensitive information that they do not wish to divulge, you are likely to create a feeling of resentment towards the team's management. If this is the case, maybe you should ask why the team members are feeling this way. It could be a strong indication that the management of the team in question may need to be re-appraised and adjusted.

At minivation, we ask whether this is a professional network as this provides a better understanding of the type of network with which we are dealing. For example, LinkedIn is most likely to be for professional use while Facebook is often a mix of personal and professional, as is Twitter. Of course, some team members may have personal and professional accounts that they keep separate. Remember, you are trying to gauge likely support for the campaign so you must decide whether or not personal numbers in this mini-audit are required.

It must also be stressed that this information should be kept securely and is a guide only. It is not a totally reliable method, but it should provide some reassurance as to the kinds of numbers the campaign can expect. It also provides some indication, no matter how rough, of how much will be needed from each social network member for the raise to reach its goal.

For example, let's imagine you are raising £1,000 and the social network support is 500 (as calculated earlier). Then you will need to persuade each network member to fund the campaign with a minimum of £2.

In this scenario the tiered rewards we saw earlier in table 2.3.2 and 2.3.3 will need to be adjusted so the minimum reward tier will be £2 for a "thank you", not £1 as it is now. That's double the original ask for that tier. But the good news is that it will need fewer people to pledge at this level. You have now doubled the impact of each pledge at this tier which means you now need half the number of pledges to reach the same level of raise.

However this may also mean double the work. Gaining crowdconsent at £1 may be a lot easier than gaining that consent at £2. Think carefully before committing either way – a campaign at this stage is about trade-offs and using your research you should be in a position to make sound judgments on these types of issues.

This also serves to show why it so essential to get as much information as possible and then to apply this information to the practical management of the campaign. Never assume you know the figures (or any other detail for that matter) and never just make up figures for the planning of your campaign. They should always be based on some concrete information that you have researched and understood.

TEAM ESSENTIALS

Creating and maintaining high standards in a team are important in any project but when the project is so open and exposed to public scrutiny, the need for standards to be maintained is even more important. Here we highlight 10 essential points that will help maintain a healthy balance in your team:

- First, campaign management must be genuinely caring, likeable, and at the same time, provide a strong sense of knowing what they are doing and where this project is heading. They must also be able to keep their heads and stay calm when the unexpected arises.
- As well as the above, the team must be given a clear sense of what the aims and goals of the campaign are. This may sound obvious, but we have encountered this problem before when the management of a campaign failed to make sure the team knew and understood the vision that was being created (see section 1.7, p86).
- All the team members must therefore share the values and expectations of the campaign. They must all be 'on the same page' and want to achieve success through a common understanding of the principles and rules that guide the campaign.

- These principles and rules can be interpreted to a degree and may need to be adjusted if the campaign calls for it. But if this is the case, the team members should be consulted and allowed a chance to influence any changes in direction the campaign may need to make. So a certain degree of flexibility is needed from each member.
- If things are changing or evolving as the campaign is being planned, or even when it's live, then the team needs to be open and accepting of other people's ideas. Conflict and trying to apportion blame for situations will soon take up a lot of valuable time. Personalities will, and do, clash, that's a part of life, but trying to create as open a culture as possible in the campaign will mean these situations will hopefully be few and far between.
- Through the open culture created early in the construction of a team there should be respect and warmth for one another. Crowdfunding can be great fun and really exciting when it comes together. It is also a massive learning curve for team members new to crowdfunding.
- The campaign management must earn respect from a team, so ensure that you do what you say you will do and make it clear if you cannot keep a promise to the team or individual members.
- Do not hide things, if the team really is behind you they will try to find answers and solve problems for the campaign and other members.
- Listen to your team. They are individuals and, as such, they probably have an understanding or can see things from a different angle than you may be able to. Take on board what they have to say and make sure they know you are listening and not just paying them lip service.
- Never take things for granted. Try to maintain a culture of open playfulness where it is ok to take risks and ask questions about everything.

This list is not exhaustive and there are many great books out there on teams and team building, but when it comes to campaigning in the crowdfunding sector we find setting out these ground rules from the outset helps set the tone for the team and also provides some kind of guidance as to the type of team they are joining or creating.

After all, team building is a highly motivating activity that, when done right, can bring with it enormous rewards for all those involved. In crowdfunding this counts, as the public will often pick up on the positive vibe a good team can generate.

Just as a listener can tell you are smiling when you speak to someone on the telephone without seeing your face, crowds can pick up on signals (team cohesion, tension) across all communication channels.

So once in a while, remind the team of the aims and objectives of the campaign, it does no harm and may even help the campaign stay on track.

TASK 17: TEAM

IDENTIFY WHO WOULD BE INCLUDED IN YOUR IDEAL TEAM.

WHAT INCENTIVES WILL YOU OFFER TO ATTRACT THEM TO THE TEAM?

REALISTICALLY, WHEN DO YOU NEED TO CREATE THIS TEAM?

HOW WILL YOU IMPLEMENT EACH OF THE 10 GUIDELINES GIVEN EARLIER?

2.5

AIMS AND OBJECTIVES

If you are not clear about the aims and objectives of your campaign then the chances are the crowd will react negatively towards your project. Plus, as we learned previously, the team working on the campaign will soon start to experience low morale. Once this happens it is very difficult to re-energize a team.

But what are aims and objectives?

This question is a very common one and we have heard several definitions from people over the years. Perhaps the clearest way to consider these is to think that the vision you are attempting to create has:

- An aim – a result that specific activities and plans are intended to achieve

- An objective – an overall or bigger end result that comes from meeting your aims

All projects need clearly-defined aims that will help them reach the bigger objective or goal that they are seeking to achieve. Aims therefore can be many smaller activities that all help to reach some bigger mission (the objective). Figure 2.5.1 is a good representation of this:

FIGURE 2.5.1: AIMS LEADING TO OBJECTIVES

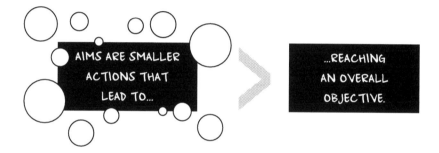

We can see on the left of figure 2.5.1 all the smaller tasks or activities (represented by the small circles) that need to be done in order for the overall objective to be achieved. A campaign therefore needs to be both clear about the little steps (the aims) and how they fit into the bigger vision of the campaign (the objective).

Without this clarity, team members and management will be unsure of what action they will need to take; this in turn will mean very slow progress being made on the campaign. Carefully planning everything is fine, but if the progress is too slow, team motivation may become a problem.

Another major issue, if aims and objectives are unclear, concerns the overall direction in which the team is meant to be heading. This is very important as, without clarity, the whole thing will quickly fall apart because no one will know what they are supposed to be doing.

The opposite is also true; providing a clear vision and strategy will make planning much more focused and the campaign will be understood by all members. They will know how what they do fits with the bigger picture and helps to create that end vision.

So far, we have looked inwards, at the team. A final issue with unclear aims and objectives is external and concerns the crowd. If objectives are unclear to the team members who are supposed to be creating the campaign, how can you expect the external crowd to understand what the campaign is attempting to achieve?

There is only one (simple) answer to this: you can't!

Trust and clarity are essential for the success of any campaign, you can have low levels of either and the campaign may succeed, but this success is going to be much more difficult for you to achieve without trust and a clear message.

FIGURE 2.5.2: TRUST / MESSAGE NEXUS IN CROWDFUNDING COMMUNICATIONS

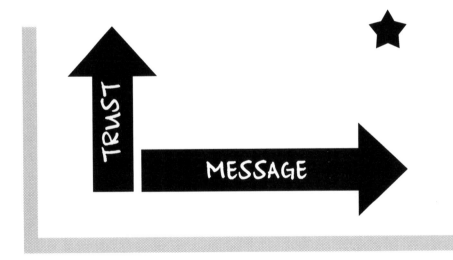

Figure 2.5.2 demonstrates this well. On the left axis is trust and on the bottom axis is the campaign message. Both should be as high as possible on each of the axes with the optimal position represented by the star in the top right corner. The star represents a campaign with a message that is clearly communicated and with aims and objectives that can be understood by the crowd; thus funders trust the campaign because they understand the vision that is being created and that the team can deliver this. With these two critical elements synchronized the campaign is in a much better position to achieve its objectives (reaching incremental aims until the objective is reached).

This builds on the concepts we encountered in section 1.4. Most ideas in crowdfunding are connected and often support one another. Look back at the CPP in section 1.6 (p82) and these connections will become more obvious as your team start mapping out the campaign on a single sheet.

TASK 18: AIMS AND OBJECTIVES

WHAT WILL BE THE AIMS AND OBJECTIVES OF YOUR CAMPAIGN?

HOW WILL YOU ENSURE TRUST AND A CLEAR MESSAGE ARE EMBEDDED IN THE CAMPAIGN?

HOW WILL YOU CLARIFY THE AIMS AND OBJECTIVES FOR THE TEAM?

2.6

RESPONSIBILITIES

Clarity for those on the inside of the campaign is an essential ingredient as we saw in section 2.4. To help with clarity, it is worth taking time to assign responsibilities for the campaign to various members of the team.

This could be codified in a written document and made an official element of the campaign or, as is often the case with smaller teams, it could be tacit knowledge that is not written down in a formal document even though every member of the team understands their role and what is expected of them.

Problems can quite quickly be blown out of proportion when disputes over roles and responsibilities surface within a team, so even with smaller teams it is worth writing out a simple overview of what is expected of each member and the things they are responsible for managing.

By doing this early on in the planning stages, you are preventing possible disputes and it will help you when you have to communicate the team's skills, expertise and responsibilities to outsiders, especially the platforms and then the crowd.

Remember that the crowd will want to know who the team members and what they know, plus how well-connected they are. This could be an opportunity to audit this information and to make sure that the campaign can communicate it efficiently to the crowd.

An easy way of doing this and of initiating the audit process we encountered in section 2.4 is to ask each member to put together a 400-word biography about their past experience and their connections.

While 400 words each will be too long for most platforms, it will start the ball rolling and get team members to think about their skill-sets and their networks (which might be beneficial to the campaign). It is often much easier to edit information than it is to create it from scratch – especially when you are writing something as personal as a biography of team members.

This information also needs to fit the needs of the campaign. One way to do this is to use the RAW method. RAW is an acronym for Responsibility, Ability and Who. Teams can use this to determine the responsibilities are and who can best fulfil these.

To complete a RAW audit, establish the aim of each role, then think about the needs of the campaign. What are the responsibilities this person will be expected to take on to meet these needs? Next, consider the abilities this person will need to have to meet these needs; is there a background in certain subjects or specific experience that will help them?

Lastly, decide who in the team will be the best 'fit' with these first two criteria.

This can then be mapped into a table as shown in 2.6.1. Note how, the boxes for 'responsibilities' and 'abilities' are quite large while the 'who' box is divided into three. It is really important that the person allocated the role is happy with this. It may be that you have the perfect fit in terms of a person's abilities but this individual is uncomfortable or unhappy with performing this role. For this reason, try to earmark at least three people who might be suitable and if your first choice does not accept the allocated role you then have other possibilities open to you.

TABLE 2.6.1: THE RAW MODEL

AIM:		
RESPONSIBILITIES	ABILITIES	WHO

Maintaining a happy team is vital in any project where people work together but perhaps even more important in crowdfunding because the project and the team are so public, everything is in the public domain and open to scrutiny by the crowd. If a team member is unhappy about certain aspects of their role or the campaign it may be picked up by the crowd. To avoid this, follow these simple rules ensure team members are:

- happy with their allocated roles
- clear about their responsibilities
- prepared to answer questions in a timely way about campaign aspects
- given sufficient time to fulfil their role

- capable of fulfilling this role to the necessary standard
- clear how their role fits into the bigger campaign picture

TASK 19: RAW

IDENTIFY THE ROLES THE CAMPAIGN NEEDS TO FULFIL.
NOW COMPLETE A RAW TABLE FOR EACH ROLE.

2.7

PROJECT FUNDING MODELS

Crowdfunding is suffering an identity crisis, not in the public domain, but within the industry itself. Some insiders would prefer to use the title 'tribefunding' to describe crowdfunding while others prefer to use 'online investment vehicle' to describe their crowdfunding activities. In this publication, as you have probably gathered by now, we prefer to use crowdfunding.

There are essentially five models of crowdfunding, and to make things easier to understand, we developed the acronym DREIM, as mentioned earlier, which stands for:

- Donation
- Reward
- Equity
- Interest
- Mixed

For projects (as opposed to personal finance, as we saw in figure 1.2.1, p27 and 1.2.2, p30) the models could be thought of as presented in figure 2.7.1:

FIGURE 2.7.1: REPRESENTATION OF THE CROWDFUNDING MODELS FOR PROJECTS

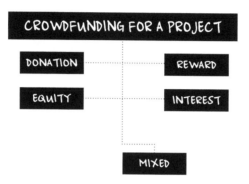

As the models move further away from the headline box ('crowdfunding for a project') so they tend to be more complex. So it follows that 'donation' is the easiest model to comprehend followed by 'reward' and things start to get more complex with 'equity' and 'interest' models.

Very few campaigns will need, or even desire, to use all the models and generally they serve quite different markets and purposes. However, minivation has helped campaigns that were planning to use two models consecutively, which we call a 'mixed' model.

Each one of the models represents a different way of using crowdfunding and some even have sub-models. It is really the legal framework and the needs of your project that determine which models are available for your project.

Most people seem to think of 'reward' when they think of crowdfunding and this is probably due to the amount of coverage that platforms like

Indiegogo and Kickstarter (both using the 'reward' model) get in the popular media. They tend to attract the lion's share of attention which is perhaps a reflection of their marketing and PR skills rather than the platform per se.

This section aims to help you understand that there are different models available and certain platforms are dedicated to certain models. UK examples of each will be given below as we introduce each one separately using the acronym DREIM.

For a comprehensive list of the platforms in the UK associated with crowdfunding, visit the 'listed' page at www.minivation.org.[32] This list is a straightforward division of the crowdfunding platforms in to their models, which act as headings. This list is fully linked and if you click on the name of the platform, a new tab opens on that platform's site.

This list goes a little further and also introduces some syndicate platforms that act like crowdfunding platforms (although actually they are closed to the crowd unless members meet certain criteria).

Using the DREIM acronym each model is introduced below.

DONATION

Of the five models, perhaps the simplest to understand is the donation model. This relies on basic philanthropy, whereby people donate money for a good cause. They are left with the warm glow of knowing they have done something positive, normally with some kind of social value. For example, within the arts, this has traditionally been represented by the concept of the sponsor, or patron, of a certain artist or field of creative work.

There are many of these in crowdfunding, perhaps the most well-known in the UK are JustGiving, Spacehive and Virgin Money; all are dedicated to social or community causes and are quite straightforward to use.

Donation is a growth area for crowdfunding and there are several mixed platforms emerging:

PROS	CONS
• Easy to understand • High visibility platforms • Platforms offer lots of great advice • Very broad range of causes accepted	• Needs careful planning • Mostly for charities or social causes • Can be difficult to mix models

REWARD

As mentioned in the introduction to this section, the reward model is the model which most comes to mind when people think about crowdfunding. The crowd makes a pledge to the project for some value (normally money) and the project offers them something in return – perhaps a poster or piece of merchandise.

The reward model is represented well on both sides of the Atlantic by Kickstarter and Indiegogo. But there are plenty of our own home-grown UK sites, like Bloom Venture Catalyst in Edinburgh and Crowdfunder in Exeter. Both of these platforms support artists and the creative industries across the UK.

For authors, there is a special model dedicated to getting your book published called Unbound. In this model, the crowd agrees to contribute money to the campaign if it wishes to see an idea for a book turned into reality.

PROS	CONS
• Easy to understand basics	• Needs very careful planning
• High visibility platforms	• Costing of rewards need special attention
• Platforms offer lots of great advice	• Can be difficult to get featured
• Very broad range of projects accepted	• Competitive environment
• Can be easier to mix models	

EQUITY

In this model, the project's management offers the crowed a share of the organization behind the project. This means the crowd members get to share any profits or sell their shares once the project becomes successful. Equally, of course, the crowd members could end up not making any returns or even losing the money they invested. This can escalate to even more money if the crowd is liable for any debts incurred by the enterprise in which members have invested.

This model is the most risky because the crowd is being asked to back a project that is new and often not yet proven in the market (technically this is called 'ex-ante'). In other words, it has a high chance of failure. For this reason, the team behind the campaign, and the idea itself, are both essential elements that need to be carefully presented to the crowd.

The best advice if you are planning an equity model campaign is to look at other campaigns, particularly how they present their teams and the types of question they are being asked by the crowd. Then pre-crowdfund the campaign to make sure the funders properly understand the vision being created.

When you offer equity, you will also need legal help to ensure everything is correct for you and the investors. This costs money and takes time to organize, but the good news is that most platforms will offer this as part of their service; sometimes the price can be added to the raise which obviously reduces the initial outlay for applicants.

Pledgers in this model (investors, if you like) will generally be looking for growth businesses that they can scale-up and sell at some future time; this is called an 'exit'. A small craft producer who works from their garage is not the kind of business these investors will normally consider.

Equity model crowdfunding platforms can also specialize in different types of project they list. For example, Seedrs is for very early start-ups, Crowd Mission specializes in social enterprises and Crowdcube specializes in both start-ups and growing businesses that need money to expand.

There are other options, and it is best to have a good look at each of these before deciding which platform is best for your project. Check your platform is a member of an official association which will regulate it and ensure it is trustworthy (in the UK, the FCA deals with these platforms).

PROS	CONS
• Savvy crowds use this model	• Requires even more careful planning
• High visibility platforms available	• Think about future needs of project
• Platforms offer lots of great advice	• Platforms can block updates
• Very broad range of projects accepted	• Government policies may change
• Platforms may have own legal papers	• Legal structures may be restricted
• SEIS/EIS may be available (see 1.2)	

INTEREST

This model is like getting a loan from a bank, except here you get the loan from the crowd. On regular dates you pay back the loan with a little interest, just like you would to a bank or any other lender. Most platforms are regulated (as with the equity model) by the FCA in the UK and will require two years' of audited accounts from the organization. This acts as a deterrent to fraudsters and provides evidence of trading activity.

Generally, the rates of interest may be a little higher than those offered by high street banks. The headline numbers might look the same, but you need to consider fees charged by the crowdfunding platform and the payment processor. This all adds up.

The interest model can be more flexible and a little quicker than the high street banks, but this really depends on the planning that has gone into the campaign prior to the live stage and the crowd's willingness to crowdconsent which can be affected by the risk rating the platform decides to give to the project. They can use their own means of working this out, for example Bank To The Future uses traditional methods combined with your social media score (they take into account your social media presence and use this in their assessments).

Interest models can also specialize in particular types of projects like Abundance Generation and Trillion Fund, both of which focus on renewables, while Funding Knight and Rebuilding Society have a very wide range of projects they accept on their platforms.

PROS	CONS
• Savvy crowds use this model	• Still needs planning
• High visibility platforms available	• Platforms can block updates
• Platforms offer lots of great advice	• Rates can be higher than banks
• Very broad range of projects accepted	• Two years accounts normally required
• Can be more flexible than the banks	• Risk ratings decided by platform
• Can get a quicker decision than with banks	

MIXED

A mixed crowdfunding model is just as it sounds: a mix of models. For example, the Crowdbnk platform offers you the chance of a reward or an equity campaign. But again, all the issues mentioned earlier need to be considered before you crowdfund your project through this type of model.

There are advantages to the mixed model if you are hoping to stage more than one campaign. For example, if a project is hoping to raise awareness and test the market through a reward campaign followed later by a bigger equity (or interest) raise then this is perfect because the campaign's management will have already developed and nurtured a relationship with that platform. Starting a new campaign on the platform for a different type of raise will be much smoother as the two management teams know each other and have an element of trust.

Again, these platforms can specialize in different types of project. Eco Propagator is dedicated to renewables while We Say We Pay is dedicated to social causes and Bank To The Future and Crowdbnk are much wider-ranging in the types of projects they allow on their platforms.

PROS	CONS
• Savvy crowds use this model	• Each model is different
• High visibility platforms available	• Needs proper planning for each stage
• Platforms offer lots of great advice	• Platforms can block updates
• Very broad range of projects accepted	• Rates can be higher than banks
• Can be more flexible than the banks	• Two years accounts normally required
• Can get a quicker decision than with banks	• Risk ratings can be decided by platform
	• Can be a competitive environment
	• Crowd apathy hard to overcome
	• Legal structures may be restricted

TASK 20: AUDIT YOUR MODEL

CONSIDERING EACH CROWDFUNDING MODEL IN TURN, OUTLINE THE ADVANTAGES AND DISADVANTAGES FOR YOUR CAMPAIGN.

NOW CHOOSE A MODEL MOST APPROPRIATE TO YOUR CAMPAIGN AND WRITE A 200-WORD JUSTIFICATION OF THIS MODEL (DO NOT EXCEED 200 WORDS).

LAST, PRODUCE A PRESENTATION OF YOUR FINDINGS YOU WOULD BE HAPPY TO SHOW YOUR TEAM.

2.8

CHOOSING A PLATFORM

Choosing the right platform may seem an obvious thing for the management of a campaign, but it needs careful consideration. It never fails to trouble the team at minivation how many campaigns are 'designed' for platforms like Kickstarter and Indiegogo (both US -owned) with no consideration of other platforms or, as we saw in the previous section, any consideration of alternative models.

Some campaign managers seem blinded by the media coverage of Kickstarter and Indiegogo and fail to see the equally effective platforms here in the UK. So (as mentioned earlier) to help make choosing easier and to help support the UK crowdfunding eco-system, minivation has put together a basic list of UK platforms grouped by the type of model they use. This page can be found at www.minivation.org (go to the 'listed' page).

At the time of writing (late 2014), the list comprised more than 90 different UK platforms from which to choose, covering all the DREIM models. However, having such a wide choice can be daunting.

Perhaps the best advice we have given applicants is to try and trace previous campaign management teams and speak to them about their experiences.

We often find that applicants of both successful and failed campaigns are more than happy to speak about their experiences of campaigning in general, and the platforms, more narrowly. This can often be really inspirational for the management team of any campaign.

As well as networking with other campaign management teams, an assessment of the platforms of which you like the 'feel' and 'look' is vital. This can be done via an audit helping you to make a decision, because you will have now collected both subjective opinions from previous management and objective information about the platforms. In simple terms, this means you are in a much stronger position to make a decision about the right platform for your project.

Pre-crowdfunding can also add huge value in the search for the perfect platform. Pre-crowdfunding means the community can add comments and vote on your campaign and members may even be able to help you decide which platform is most appropriate for your campaign. Remember, crowdfunding may not even be necessary, business angels or mentors may approach campaign management and offer their resources away from crowdfunding. But bear in mind that crowdfunding is not just about getting the money.

It can be the case that after all this work, researching and networking, you end up choosing the original platform you identified. There is nothing wrong with this, at least you will be much more confident that this is the right one for you and the right space for you to attract your audience.

The importance of auditing both the team and the campaign has already been introduced. Using this concept for the platforms will boost your confidence when it comes to making a choice. This auditing process is slightly different in that it also includes a SWOT analysis (see 1.7, p86) to help the decision process; doing so will help you identify strengths and weaknesses that may not have been obvious before. Remember, time spent on this type of thing early on – before you go live – will save a lot of sleepless nights and headaches when you do eventually go public.

One last issue we need to bring up now is the nature of the platforms. Many applicants have commented on the way some platforms have controlled their campaigns. This has ranged from delaying updates on the main page to even suspending a campaign mid-flow, sometimes with no justification for doing so.

This is the kind of tacit knowledge that can prove extremely difficult to trace or find out until it's too late, so speaking to previous campaign management can really help you get to grips with the overall picture of the platforms and the way they have dealt with previous applicants.

By speaking with fellow applicants, and getting their angle on the platform and the way their campaign was handled, you can start to build a picture of the platform. Of course, you may need to take any information with a 'pinch of salt' as some applicants will have a perception of a negative situation that they, themselves, may have blown out of proportion.

In an extreme case, they may even be to blame for a situation, about which they are embarrassed. This means they might not be forthcoming with all the facts behind the way they were treated. It is for you to decide how much you can depend on fellow applicants' tips and advice with reference to the platforms (or indeed any aspect of crowdfunding).

TASK 21: CHOICES

CHOOSE YOUR PLATFORM.

NOW WRITE A 400-WORD JUSTIFICATION FOR USING THIS PLATFORM (YOU CAN INCLUDE BULLET POINTS). MAKE SURE YOU HAVE CONSIDERED ALTERNATIVE PLATFORMS AND CONDUCTED A SWOT ANALYSIS.

PRODUCE A PRESENTATION OF YOUR FINDINGS YOU WOULD BE HAPPY TO SHOW YOUR TEAM.

2.9

SOCIAL MEDIA

We live in a world in which, more than ever before, we are connected to individuals with whom we may never meet in real time, never have a chat over a cup of tea, about the weather or any number of mundane issues that affect our everyday lives. The internet has enabled a remarkable thing to happen: we can get news, instantly, of loved ones, wars, economics, deaths and marriages from anywhere in the world as long we have access to the infrastructure that enables the World Wide Web to function.

Trade has been enabled too. With auction sites and wholesale sites, we can now trade with one another at remarkable speed and with remarkable results. This has affected almost every field and is in constant flux as new ways of doing things, connecting and trading are emerging (just look at crowdfunding itself).

But perhaps more importantly than any other change enabled through this connectivity is the democratization of cultures. This was touched upon at the beginning of this book, it is the concept of living in an interactive culture.

Radio is a good example of what we mean by this. In the past, record companies sent out their people to track down new talent and report this back to their headquarters. If a band was lucky, it would be set some sort of task and then signed a contract that meant its music would be distributed and publicized through the record company.

DJs at radio stations were briefed and sent copies of the music that was produced. DJs also had a say (to a degree) in what did and what did not get played on their shows. Fans heard the music and showed approval by purchasing the music from retail stores.

This was a one-way concept: corporate body (production) to corporate body (wholesale) to corporate body (retail) to individual (public). But then along came the World Wide Web and remarkable things happened very fast.

Connectivity spread like wild fire across the globe. With this connectivity comes the ability to do things differently.

The price of tools for the production of cultural artefacts has fallen a lot. At the same time, pro-am started to disseminate information about how to do things and improve the cultural productions that were being attempted. Barriers to distribution, as we have already seen, have also been broken down by this new phenomenon of the World Wide Web.

These three incremental changes have had such an impact on society that older methods are already being viewed as antiquated remnants of a time of cultural dictatorship. So to summarize, three simple things happened in sequence that changed our world:

1. Cultural tools for production have grown cheaper
2. Information about techniques has been shared and is freely available

Barriers to distributing to, or contacting, individuals (or groups) have been removed

Returning to our record company example, there has been a massive change in the model the industry was used to. Now people can mix and produce their own music on turntables and recording devices in their own homes. Other people can offer tips and advice about how to get the best out of their equipment. Music can also be freely distributed among the global population.

The old methods have become redundant. Record companies no longer seek the next big act they can sign to a contract. DJs have less influence as the population turns to other sources of information and buy or access their music from freely available sites where they can stream the tunes of their choice.

Finally, the wholesale and retail 'bricks and mortar shopping environments' have given way to the sleek new websites that offer the streaming services and also the opportunity to purchase digital copies of the music from their stores.

How do we know if anything is any good?

Simple: we listen to, and participate in, online conversations with our peers via blogs, dedicated forums and social media platforms like Facebook or Twitter. This is really powerful and means that the one-way cultural model of the past is now a two-way super highway straining under all the content being distributed (mostly for free) across the World Wide Web.

We can link with the creators and chat with them, offer advice, agree with their point of view, criticize them or praise them in a number of ways. Essentially though, all this can be done online at an incredible speed. The thing is, this change is happening now, in fields that were thought untouchable by this kind of phenomenon, and crowdfunding is feeding this change.

Social media is important in crowdfunding but perhaps not for the reasons you think. Simple online conversations can help campaigns by revealing, confirming or disproving elements of a campaign.

Using social media properly can allow hidden stories to be told to your audience and communicate things that were unsaid on the campaign pages. For example, this could include the quality of new materials being used or the exploration of a new medium that is creating unexpected results.

Social media is a great way to start a dialogue with the audience with which the campaign is seeking to engage and to promote both your craft and your crowdfunding campaign in a more subtle way. Perhaps the most obvious way of doing this is through the use of updates on your campaign page or blog posts, but the power of Twitter and LinkedIn should not be underestimated. Both can act as a magnet for interest in your project and crowdfunding campaign especially when you are pre-crowdfunding. Campaigners can build significant interest before they go live, bringing to their campaign an already enthusiastic crowd as they launch and ask for the money.

Through entering this dialogue you are also creating space for a story of shared experiences to evolve. These shared stories are not necessarily related to your core campaign. This is perfectly ok, provided the stories being told are positive. They can help nurture a great deal of trust in you and your campaign which, in turn, can help people feel the warm glow of doing something good for you and the vision you represent.

This warm glow could be in the form of pledging money but equally it could be in the form of promoting your campaign and profile to others in their networks (these are all elements of crowdconsent). This in turn can generate interest that may be worth a lot more to you than a one-off pledge from the person. Even tips and advice can be offered – all of which add value generated through starting a simple online conversation.

Through this conversation there are also opportunities for value to be recognized and acknowledged. Someone may like your work and think the campaign looks really good. Equally, something is often missing when pledgers fail to identify the real value your campaign is generating. Through open discourse on social media the value aspects can emerge freely and be recognized and acknowledged by all your external followers.

Internally, too, this can help as your team becomes more aware of the value the campaign may be generating for different sectors of the network it connects. This can boost morale within a team which feeds more positivity into the campaign.

All this forms part of the hidden story that emerges as you tell people about your journey, a journey that started way back when inspiration suddenly found you and you had the initial idea for the project. A campaign page is a great place to tell this story but pre-crowdfunding and social media are even greater places to build in these hidden gems and add rich layers to the story.

There are also opportunities here for you to chat about the shared experiences that others bring with them to the discussion; what's more, this can all be done in real time, on the move and with the entire crowd at the same time.

It is important to remember that even though you are replying to one person, the response is open to the crowd. In other words, the dialogue you are having is addressed to one person but open for discussion with many.

In all the campaigns on which I have worked, I have never entered a dialogue with just one person. Although I may have responded to one person, I have, in fact, been talking to the crowd. This is significant because you want the crowd to be listening to the voice of the campaign and the message you are trying to convey.

Therefore, the message and any subsequent conversations in your campaign must follow the 'four C's' model and be;

- Coherent (understandable)
- Cohesive (gelled together and on subject - don't go off talking about other stuff)
- Concise (to the point)
- Consistent (same message and story in all you say)

Your response must be in keeping with the aims of the campaign, understandable by all and to the point.

One way to achieve this is to set out clear rules about the campaign's content before you begin. This should be planned well before the campaign starts and should include the number of updates you will make each week and the content of those updates.

To give an example, on most campaigns we work with the 80/20 rule:

- Approximately 80% of the updates will be directly about the campaign's core subject
- Approximately 20% will be about the peripheral stuff happening in the market more broadly

Let us imagine we are working with a jeweller and his campaign is running for 10 weeks and we are updating twice a week – so 20 updates in total.

This would mean 16 updates relating directly to his jewellery and the remaining four updates about the jewellery market more broadly (a new clasp, price of pewter, a competition he is thinking of entering and jewellery in cake design, or whatever).

These are common themes that emerge in our updates and, wherever possible, we include lifestyle interests (fashion, food, home and so on) in this content as this allows even more people to enter the conversation, who will hopefully engage with his campaign. In effect, what this is doing is extending the buzz beyond his core network, getting as wide exposure as possible through the conversations he is entering.

To help this, don't be afraid to connect with your network before you go live with the campaign. Spread the word and the love by telling as many people as possible about it. One way to do this is to pre-crowdfund your idea, where you get the chance to test your ideas before you go live and ask the crowd for the money. In other words, you get to polish your offer and make mistakes in a safer environment.

Getting people to support you and agree to put their money into the project via the campaign platform before you go live is a great advantage because this will lead to interest from people beyond your immediate network (friends of friends and so on).

Think about it this way: if you are creating value for people, then you have a duty to tell them about this value. You are actually doing some good by using your energy to tell people about the project and entering a conversation with them. If you like helping people then actually the best thing you can do is help them by informing them of this great new vision they can help you create. For this to happen, you need to ensure you are communicating with these networks through channels that they are happy for you to use. If you fail to check this at the outset, your message could easily be seen as yet more noise adding volume to already straining inboxes.

Checking these channels are appropriate can be an element of the audits you conduct. This will be given more coverage in section 3.

TASK 22: SOCIAL MEDIA AUDITS

AUDIT THE POTENTIAL SOCIAL MEDIA CHANNELS FOR YOUR CAMPAIGN.

NOW CREATE A LIST OF TOPICS YOU WILL WRITE ABOUT VIA THESE CHANNELS.

WRITE THE CONTENT.

GET FEEDBACK ON YOUR IDEAS AND WRITING.

SECTION 3:
ENGAGE

CONTENTS

3.1

TARGET USERS

You will often hear people talk about "target users" but this can be a deceptive term. Generally, in crowdfunding, there are often three types of target users that can be approached simultaneously, these are:

- Ambassadors
- End users, and
- Fun seekers

Each one has a different role to play in your campaign's success through the granting of crowdconsent. They also play a role beyond the crowdfunding activity when the product or service is actually on the market. Continuous engagement with these groups will help you to create a long-term relationship with them and ultimately lead to a sustainable enterprise.

But this is the longer view and these target users may also be tribal members (see section 2, p104). As in tribal consumerism, the campaign's aim should be to support members rather than sell to them.

Ambassadors are important for spreading the word. They are curators of information and can be found on most social media platforms. They are easy to spot as they are continuously writing about things from the sectors they love. They can help spread the word, they may not support you financially, but they can offer much-needed breadth of coverage of a campaign by broadcasting it to their followers. Their motivation is pure social capital.

End users are those who will actually derive a value from the use of the vision you are creating. They are obviously important as this is the crowd you most want to help you. They may, ironically, be quite poor at broadcasting or promoting the vision you are creating, because of social capital. It may be that your end users are actually the quietest group because they do not need the same bragging rights that the ambassadors are seeking. Their motivation is in the utility of the vision.

Lastly, the fun seekers are out to have a little fun, and at times learn, while surfing the various categories of crowdfunding. They tend to be savvy and engaged in one or two areas and rarely step outside these. For example some will really be into design, others the latest gadgets while others still will be into new takes on business models. Once they connect with your campaign, they tend to be quite vocal about their finds through the various social media channels they use.

It is possible that target users can be a combination of ambassador, end user and fun seeker. For example, an end user may also be an ambassador for the service or product. As we saw in section 2.2 (Research) they may also be influenced by others beyond their immediate network. Of course, they may be the influencers for others. A careful look at their social media should reveal which they are and how their crowdconsent can be gained.

It helps to know all this information because your pitch can now be focused. When writing your pitch you need to consider the product or service from two perspectives: the features of the vision you want to create and the benefits this vision will deliver. These benefits should be aligned with the motivation of the target user.

By separating these two areas, the pitch can address the one essential question individuals will want to know before they give their consent – that is: *"What is in it for me?"*

This is a deceptively simple question. Yet it is the single most important question when writing a pitch. Think about it this way: if you take a car in for a service, and you are not technically-minded or interested in the workings of cars, would you want to know all the details of the activities the mechanic had performed on your vehicle?

Probably not!

What you would like to know is that the vehicle is safe, is less likely to break down and should not need any further exceptional expense in the next few months, not for repairs anyhow. The mechanic can tell you this and you would probably be happy.

In effect, what the mechanic has informed you about are the benefits of the servicing, not all the details about the changing of the battery in the key fob; the oil that was overdue and really thick black with metal particles in it; or about the left front tyre which was under-pressure; or for that matter the right headlight which was two whole degrees lower on full beam than it should have been…

You get the picture I'm sure. The point is that the pitch needs to be approached from two angles right from the start, the features and the benefits. An easy way to do this is to start by writing in a two-column grid the features and then the benefits, as shown in table 3.1.1:

TABLE 3.1.1: FEATURES VERSUS BENEFITS

FEATURES	BENEFITS
Changed key fob battery	Central locking works again
Changed the oil	Engine sounds quieter
Changed the tyres	Uses less fuel
Adjusted front headlight	Can see much better at night

The wording you use in your pitch should reflect the benefits and a good technique borrowed from the sales sector is to start by writing the 'sales message' first. The sales message is about identifying the problem you are able to solve for the potential customer and then demonstrating that you can deliver on that promised solution. Once you have got the sales message right it can be used on all your promotional materials (flyers, for example) that potential customers get to see.

For more detail on the sales message see 3.5 (p200).

TASK 23: DESCRIBE TARGET USERS

DESCRIBE YOUR TARGET USERS WITH IMAGES AND TEXT.

THESE CAN BE SIMPLE STICK FIGURES, IMAGES COPIED AND PASTED OR STAR FIGURES.

THE TEXT SHOULD DETAIL WHO THEY ARE.

3.2

PRODUCT OR SERVICE?

By the time you come to present the campaign to the crowd and go live (ask for the money) you should be very clear about what it is you are asking crowdconsent for – it is either a product, a service or a combination of these.

What may be less obvious is the value you are creating through the campaign. This is because value can be many different things to many different people. It also depends on who you ask and their individual perspective on things. To give you an example: imagine you are producing a piece of theatre. What value does a theatre production provide?

You would probably struggle to answer unless you knew the genre of production, the audience it was targeting, the time of day or night it was being performed and many more aspects besides. It would also depend on your perspectives or even your role at work. For example, a member of the local parish council would most likely refer to the value of having a diverse range of ethnicities engaging with the production, or even the promotional aspects of the local area through the play.

Ask the director of the play and she might respond that the audience diversity and promotional aspects of the production are important. She might equally suggest that peer recognition for her skills as a director are also important value points that should be considered.

Ask an actor in the production and their value might be having a job, fulfilling a burning ambition to act, heightening their stage profile or even simply adding to their repertoire as an actor by being challenged in this role.

For the audience, the value they seek could be entertainment, education, to be challenged or simply to experience the event for what it is – a technical production.

Immediately, there are several ways in which the production could be measured and the impact assessed. Through this assessment, the value that is being created can be gauged in some way. Value then changes depending on the person you are asking and this is important because unless you understand the value that the target users are seeking it will be quite difficult for the campaign to gain traction and perhaps, more importantly, to keep that traction going for the duration of the campaign.

Be clear from the outset what value you want to create and how you are going to measure this value creation and the impact this will have. These aspects will be immensely helpful for the updates and broadcasts you will be making during the life of the campaign.

TASK 24: VALUE

WHAT IS THE VALUE YOU ARE CREATING THROUGH THIS CAMPAIGN?

WRITE A FEW SENTENCES SUMMARIZING THE VALUE.

3.3

REWARDS

This was given coverage earlier, but the importance of the rewards you are offering is worth reiterating, especially if you are using the donation, equity, interest or mixed models. This is because, even if you are not using the reward model, you can still offer some token reward (a gifted thank you) for crowdconsent.

Some platforms may even encourage you to do so. This is fine, but do not get bullied into offering rewards just for the sake of it. The types of reward we are suggesting here are those seen earlier in section 2.3, where we defined the rewards in terms of their atoms and / or their bits.

Random gifts of thanks are fine but why would you bother unless they were really going to help motivate the crowd to give their consent to the campaign?

Mugs, keyrings, USB memory sticks and a whole range of other things are available for you to offer. But offering a keyring to a crowd investing in an equity share of a start-up is unlikely to be the key (no pun intended) factor in crowdconsent being given to the project.

In fact, it could even have the opposite effect. A random offer like this is not well thought through and the expense of the key ring production and delivery is another cost added to the this operation. The crowd could see this as a negative thing.

On the other hand, a small thank you gift (which is really what we are talking about here) that is matched (or fits) with the project in some way might be appreciated more. It will, in itself, probably not be the reason for the crowdconsent being given, but a nice thank you is often warmly received rather than rejected.

Inspiration for your own gifted thank you can come from almost anywhere and using well proven ideas with a twist of your own can really add a little sparkle to your pitch. However you do need to avoid apathy among the crowd.

If your pitch is full of descriptions of how fantastic the rewards are it will pretty quickly become a bit boring for the reader. So introduce them, but keep them to a minimum. The reader really wants to know what the benefits of the project are for them, and the wider value that is being created, and this should be the focus of any pitch in crowdfunding not the rewards themselves.

STRETCH GOALS

As discussed earlier, stretch goals are ways to add greater value to a project's crowdfunding campaign by offering something extra than was originally intended or promised.

Imagine that the goal is to raise £30,000 for an innovative new method of re-using the frames of old reading glasses but with new lenses that can be popped in without the need for an optician or specialist. Let's call it 'Popped Lenses'.

Popped Lenses launches a 90-day campaign, and within 30 days it reaches its £30,000 target. The team still has 60 days of campaigning left – it would normally have a choice now, either to take the £30,000 and its create vision (Popped Lenses) or stick with the campaign and add additional promises for anyone adding money beyond their £30,000.

This could be the option for a second pair of lenses for example. Popped Lenses will get the money – it has secured the £30,000 initial target and will not lose this amount if it fails to reach a stretch goal.

What the team is doing with the stretch goals is adding an additional incentive for the crowd to back the campaign further and create something even better than the original vision. If it doesn't reach its stretch goal, it is still happy as the team has reached the £30,000 original target.

Problems exist with this in terms of perceptions of fairness; making it fair for the original members of the crowd that have already backed the project. Will they feel hard done by if they cannot get the extra thing you are offering?

If you add additional 'bells and whistles' to the vision you are creating, you will have to meet this demand and spend time producing or creating stuff that may not have been on your radar when you originally set out on this path. Capacity is the real key to this. Ask yourselves: *"Can we actually fulfil the additional requirements in the stretch goals - is there enough time and resources to enable this to happen?"* It is a tricky decision that needs consideration before you go live, but even then, things can come to light that can change the stretch goals. For example, a recent drinking vessel campaign which reached its target and decided to offer some stretch goals set the goals that the crowd had asked for through the update forum on the site.

This meant that the crowd was fully engaged with the entrepreneur and the team behind the project and able to influence the stretch goals directly. It also meant the project's management team was viewed as really responsive to the crowd's desires and needs.

The lesson is not to fear setting stretch goals but, at the same time, to bear in mind that you need to be flexible with them and open to suggestions from the crowd. You may have some brilliant ideas, but the crowd may equally have something in mind that is more desirable or has a stronger intrinsic value.

End users are, after all, the people who will be consuming or using the product or service most frequently, so it makes sense to get their ideas and input on any adjustments or improvements you are planning to offer. This is really an opportunity for the campaign to fuse crowdsourcing with crowdfunding and adding value to the product or service as a result.

We have already highlighted the benefits of pre-crowdfunding but it is worth remembering that, through a pre-crowdfunding campaign, these kinds of problems may have already been ironed out. This will result in you and the team being much more confident that the extras offered are a good fit with the product/service being created and the crowd's expectations. The campaign will have been tested before a live audience and their input used to improve the offer when it goes live.

Engagement at this level can also bring many more benefits to the campaign. This is because people who have had some sort of input in an idea are more likely to tell others - adding fuel to that elusive but essential buzz frenzy.

TASK 25: STRETCH GOALS

REWARD MODEL:
WHAT STRETCH GOALS WILL BE OFFERED?

OTHER MODEL:
WHAT ADDITIONAL *THANK YOU* REWARDS WILL/COULD BE OFFERED?

BUZZ

In contemporary marketing circles 'buzz' tends to be viewed as a slightly dated phenomenon. But in crowdfunding, it is just as important today as it has always been; it is necessary and part of the DNA of the process. This is because the whole process is social and relies on crowdconsent.

Buzz is created when people chatter and talk about things that excite them. Sometimes referred to as 'word-of-mouth', buzz can be infectious, but it can also die out almost as soon as it is created. For campaign management, this latter situation can be quite problematic. Buzz must be sustained for the duration of the campaign (or at least until funding targets are met).

So how do you maintain buzz over the duration of the campaign?

The truth is nobody really knows. There are lots of books out there on both buzz and word-of-mouth marketing, but when it comes to crowdfunding the only rule that can be applied is to keep the conversation going with the influencers you identified earlier.

Take control of the pattern of the updates (when, how, where) and maintain this throughout the duration of the campaign's life. This will also allow the hidden stories (see section 2.9, p168) to emerge and reinforce the conversations you are having. These can help maintain buzz around the campaign but it takes stamina and effort to keep this momentum.

A simple update planner can be created to ensure that the team does not run out of steam and members are able to maintain a dialogue with the audience. This update planner can, for the most part, be pre-written and supplemented with real-time events and activities associated with the campaign. A typical schedule is shown in table 3.3.1.

This is for six weeks but there is no reason it cannot be extended to accommodate any length of campaign. The topics are the subjects to write about; these should be kept as broad-ranging as possible and be fairly vague in terms of the actual topics you are going to be discussing. The synopsis is a basic overview of what will be said in the update.

More detail can be written out in full in a separate document and this whole exercise can be repeated for all channels (Facebook, Twitter, blogs and even the update pages). By producing this kind of template, a focus is provided that can help maintain the energy in the communications with the crowd necessary to sustain any buzz.

TABLE 3.3.1: A TYPICAL UPDATE PLANNER SCHEDULE

TOPIC	SYNOPSIS
1	
2	
3	
4	
5	
6	

Campaigns may not deem this necessary or they may create a template similar to the one above and never use the content. That's fine as long as the communication is continuing. There is nothing worse than suddenly realizing no updates have been produced for a few weeks and management cannot think of anything 'interesting' to say or report. But if this does happen, then maybe management should consider their commitment to the project.

The best use of this template is to have it as the main plan while also keeping the buzz alive around the campaign by communicating the real time stuff that's happening. This planned sequence of updates will take a lot of the strain out of the 'live' stage of the campaign.

Questions from the crowd can also help to create a sense of buzz and excitement around the campaign. Feeding real-time events and happenings to the crowd is great but if these can be created in response to a direct question, or conversation, from the crowd then so much the better. It provides a personal touch which is felt not just by the individual who has asked the question, but by all who have given their consent or are just browsing.

Uless you are the type of person who can just type out responses in no time and make them appropriate to the campaign, this type of thing takes time to do. A well-composed response can be worth a lot to the campaign.

Generally, this applies more to donation and reward models, as in the equity and interest models the crowd's questions tend to be much more focused on the business side of things and this can mean some searching questions being asked about the business model or team. This is not to say there is no value in creating at least a simple (as demonstrated on page 191) version of this template.

In all models, communication is the key during the live stage of any campaign. Having thought through at least some of the most likely questions the crowd could ask will help maintain a balance lacking in other campaigns where this has not been considered and things have been left more to chance.

Competition in all models is increasing dramatically and reports indicate continued growth in all crowdfunding activities for the next few years. For this reason alone, it should be obvious that campaign management needs to be as prepared as it possibly can be before launching and going live.

Campaign managers also owe it to their crowd and team to give this their best shot. You, as campaign manager, are responsible for the creation and that should be viewed as an honour, not a burden!

TASK 26: UPDATE PLANNER

COMPLETE AN UPDATE PLANNER FOR EACH CHANNEL YOUR CAMPAIGN WILL BE USING.

3.4

THE STORY

Without exception, good pitches are told like a story.

When working with minivation clients developing their crowdfunding campaign strategies, our team normally suggests starting with the same five areas to begin the creative process of story writing. These five starting points are:

1. Introduction (the setting)
2. Problem (the human need for change)
3. Solution (your economically sustainable idea which needs help)
4. Summary (a better future as a result of the impact the idea has)
5. Budgets (a clear outline of budgets and expenditure to make the impact a reality)

First, like any great story, a pitch needs to set out the context of the issues it is addressing, and then highlight the team or people behind the pitch. From here, you can start to address the main actors (the baddies, the goodies and the heroes).

Sometimes, we refer to 'the back story' of the campaign which includes all the competition in your market. Even with non-profit or community interest projects, there are always others operating in related fields, if not actually tackling the same problem you are attempting to address. This is important to map out as it will help you define where your project fits into the overall space and what it is that you offer that is special in some way. You need to define your USP (unique selling point) that will make you stand out from the rest.

By stating this early in the story, you are allowing those with an interest to stay with the pitch and learn more. Perhaps as importantly, those who have no interest in your project can also stop at this point and move on. Only a small amount of time is wasted and the campaign now has the attention of the consent-givers it needs.

Timescales within which to address the central issue can also be introduced here that should lead nicely to the problem that the campaign wishes to address. The problem is not necessarily a problem for everyone, but it should be for the core target users in the campaign. So outline the pain you feel to these users and empathize with them as you too have struggled in this area or with this issue for some time (as you announced in the introduction above).

Now you can move to the solution: what is the simple-but-effective solution you have thought of? Stay within the language confines of your audience. Do not, for example, grow overly complex with technical details. If crowd members wish to know specific complex details they can always ask you questions through the updates section of the campaign page. This can be a very effective strategy for gaining more interaction with your crowd.

Simplify the message at this stage, if people want to know more they must ask!

Your responses here can often mean extra weight is given to you as a credible person and/or team. In effect, you are sending out a stronger signal that this is a high-quality project with a team that knows its stuff.

If it is a complex area and your solution is equally complex, you will need to break down the solution so that people can understand the ideas essence or core. Remember, as you write, that the question they will need you to address is, "What is in it for me?" The answer is embedded in the solution and can now emerge.

Now summarize the whole scene for the crowd. Your background; the problem; how you came to be affected by the issue; the solution and the brighter future this solution will be able to achieve; the timeframes the crowd can expect, and any wider outcomes that could potentially happen as a result of their consent.

From here, you can set out the finances of the project: how much money you need; what it will be spent on; how it will be economically sustainable and when any future returns to the crowd can be expected.

This is a generic outline of the main pitch, but it has proved to be a very effective starting point for minivation clients. It has been applied to all sorts of areas and all kinds of business models. Once the backbone is written following the aforementioned template, then you and your team can start to refine it and make it more personalized to fit with your campaign.

Never be afraid to challenge the assumptions that will be made about your pitch from both internal members of the team and external partners. A pitch takes time to craft and is something that should be done with time to reflect and refine as it evolves.

There will probably be many drafts, many hours and many tears before a version starts to emerge with which you feel happy, a version that does the job you need it to do and motivates the crowd into giving its consent.

KNOWLEDGE CAPTURE
Often, knowledge capture is viewed as the least important aspect of a campaign and, in some ways, it probably is.

But it is still relevant because it helps with the post-campaign reflection. Crowdfunding, whether done rightly or wrongly, is a powerful means of aligning a product or service with a group of customers. Even when a campaign fails to reach its raise target, a connection (or bond) is formed with the crowd. No matter how large or small that crowd is, it is composed of customers and what has been created is a connection, one that can be nurtured into something really beneficial.

The crowdfunding customer is a working customer; these people have helped to breathe some life into the project and thus create a reality where the project has lived and breathed. They have worked to get others involved and spread the word about the project. They have gained social capital and status among their peers because you have allowed them access to the product or service. This is powerful stuff and should not be forgotten.

Any recording of this should be done methodically and accurately. Even if the raise is not met, you the applicant, your team, the customers and the platform are all heroes in this story. This should be celebrated

– and this is where knowledge capture can really define the story of the campaign once everything is over and the dust begins to settle.

There will be a permanent record for all the stakeholders to access and reflect on later. It also means that if you decide to go for it in the future there is some kind of template for you to call on to guide you. The legacy of the campaign may even be the knowledge that has been captured on the journey, something for future researchers to study and incorporate in their analysis of how crowdfunding works, or even just for friends and family as a kind of scrapbook of the experience.

On a more practical level, it will also help you to recall any events in the future. Imagine six months after the campaign has closed a journalist makes an enquiry about a certain aspect of the campaign's life. How will you remember, with any confidence, the events or sequence of events?

Knowledge capture should not be too complicated and could be in the form of a notebook, a diary or even a scrapbook. It could be text-based, image-based or both. It could be created on paper or on a computer. Knowledge capture is flexible but the benefits are enormous. The only caveat to this is that this is done thoroughly and accurately. If you decide to keep a record (because that is really what we are talking about) then keep it going for the duration. It is so disappointing for both the record keeper and the stakeholders to see an effort made at the beginning of the campaign and then see it just stop and be left hanging.

One way to do this is to keep a spare file (physical or on a computer - or both) and keep cuttings and so on in these files. Remember, though, to date these so that later, when you come to write up everything, you know the chronological sequence in which things happened.

TASK 27: STORY TELLING

1. ONLY USING GRAPHICS OF SOME KIND – SHOW THE CAMPAIGN'S STORY.

2. NOW ADD TEXT TO THE IMAGES ABOVE TO TELL A FULLER STORY.

3. NOW REMOVE THE IMAGES AND EDIT THE TEXT UNTIL A COHESIVE AND CONCISE STORY EMERGES.

3.5

THE SALES MESSAGE

A winning formula for a sales message is one that addresses the question we met above: *"What is in it for me,"* and combines all three of these elements:

I. IT SPEAKS TO YOUR TARGET USERS

To speak to your target users, you need to use language they will understand. An artist may not understand the language of a scientist researching some niche area of quantum physics and, in turn, the scientist may be lost by the language used by a surfer to describe their perfect day riding waves.

By getting the language right, we are more likely to engage the targets we want to engage. But of course, there are also dangers in this. Very specific or overly technical language may alienate the majority of the crowd and leave some people with the feeling that your vision is not something they would like to help create.

As always, it depends on the research you have conducted and who your target is, context is also very relevant here. If it is a very small, narrow and focused group then a highly technical and specific type of language might serve the campaign well to get these target users to give their consent. This is where the context can help you formulate the appropriate means of communication (see 3.7, p220), resulting in you communicating with the crowd on their level in terms that they understand to which they are willing to listen.

2. IT EMPATHIZES WITH THE PROBLEMS THEY FACE

Having got the language right and the context of the communication attuned to the target users, now you can prove to the target users how you understand their problem – perhaps you have first-hand experience of the problems they face? You understand and can share the impact this problem is having on them. Because of this you come with an insight and a solution that is both effective and appropriate to their needs.

3. IT DEMONSTRATES A SOLUTION TO THE PROBLEM

A great way to get this across to the crowd is to include referrals from people you have helped with this solution. By focusing on others with similar problems and the benefits that you were able to provide, it will demonstrate to the crowd that you are capable of delivering on the promises you are making in this campaign. Looking back to figure 2.5.2 (p150); this is the trust axis. You have communicated well through the use of language appropriate to your target users and now you are providing proof that you are trustworthy and will deliver the results they seek.

TASK 28: SALES MESSAGE

CREATE YOUR SALES MESSAGE.

WHAT PAIN DO YOUR TARGET USERS FEEL THAT YOU CAN EASE?

1. ONLY USING GRAPHICS OF SOME KIND – SHOW THE SALES MESSAGE.

2. NOW ADD TEXT TO THE IMAGES ABOVE TO GIVE A FULLER MESSAGE.

3. NOW REMOVE THE IMAGES AND EDIT THE TEXT UNTIL A COHESIVE AND CONCISE MESSAGE EMERGES.

3.6

SCRIPTS

Scripts are the written story the campaign needs in order to motivate the crowd to give its consent. Teams do this through various points of contact with the audience (which we call 'steps').

As with the story in section 3.4 and the sales message in 3.5, this section can be adapted to suit your individual campaign. Below are the main scripts any campaign in any of the models will need to consider before going live. This order is recommended by minivation, but this is down to personal taste and finding what works best for you and your team.

At minivation, we break the script writing down into the following six steps:

1. Hook
2. Main page

3. Press
4. Video
5. Updates
6. Social media

A widely recognized model to help you when writing this section is the AIDA model. The acronym AIDA stands for: Attention, Interest, Desire and Action. Keeping this sequence in mind can help to focus your writing when you approach the scripts for the first time.

It can seem a bit clinical writing to a formula in this way but by taking account of the AIDA model early in the writing process, the script's style can be edited and rewritten to match your particular campaign. Remember this is a starting rather than an end point.

TABLE 3.6.1: STEPS AND STAGE

STEPS	STAGE
1 HOOK	ATTENTION
2 MAIN PAGE	INTEREST /ACTION
3 PRESS	INTEREST/DESIRE
4 VIDEO	DESIRE/ACTION
5 UPDATES	ACTION
6 SOCIAL MEDIA	ACTION

Table 3.6.1 sets out clearly the function of each stage in the main scripts. This order is far from perfect but it does help to add cohesiveness to the writing of the content in these sections. With increasing campaign volume of varied quality, anything that can help you stand out a little and indicate a degree of quality in the market is a big advantage.

Below, we look in a little more detail at each of the six steps.

HOOK

Every campaign needs a hook. A hook is designed to entice a platform's surfers into learning more about your campaign. In general terms, this needs to be written in 20 words or fewer.

You have to condense the sales message until it makes sense and still conveys the core of the vision you are trying to create. The best tip for doing this is to look at how other campaigns have managed it. Think of it as a summary of the benefits you offer your crowd.

TASK 29: WRITE YOUR HOOK

WRITE YOUR HOOK IN 20 WORDS OR FEWER. USE EACH OF THE GRID SPACES BELOW FOR ONE WORD ONLY. IF YOU USE HYPHENS, COLONS OR SEMI-COLONS THESE MUST USE ONE SPACE.

1		2	
3		4	
5		6	
7		8	
9		10	
11		12	
13		14	
15		16	
17		18	
19		20	

MAIN PAGE

The main page is the second thing any surfer coming across your campaign will see, so it needs to be well-presented and concise. This is also where the story really gets to 'take on colour'.

The hook is a kind of black and white outline of the project while the main page (sometimes called the project page) is where the surfer really gets to read about the detail of the project and all the characters that populate this story.

The story you created in 3.4 can now be applied to the main page. As the second thing the surfers to the platform will see, it should be fairly obvious that this must connect the values being created in the campaign with the values the crowd are likely to back.

Alongside the text, it is also a good idea to include some quality images. These serve to attract the attention of the surfer/crowd and can significantly increase the length of time people actually spend looking at the campaign's main page.

The main page is also a great place to start outlining the rewards and how they fit with the offer. Most surfers will be familiar with the crowdfunding model you use, but it is always good to link things together and so repeating some information or reinforcing a message can be done here on the main page.

Most platforms will also allow you to add content and update your main page as the campaign unfolds. This is important as not all surfers will read the updates, but they may read (or at least skim over) the main page. Remember the AIDA model we introduced in section 3.6. As we saw, the purpose of AIDA is to interest a potential funder and then to motivate this person to take action. If it is really well-written then it might even persuade them to inform others in their network of the campaign, thus spreading the word further.

Whether your campaign is for-profit or a social venture of some description, the function of this page is always the same. It adds depth to the message surfers have already been exposed to in the hook. Really the bottom line here is you have their attention – now sell it to them!

PRESS

In today's 'always on' society, the media is often an underused resource but can be a really powerful means of getting your campaign's message out there and raising general awareness of the fact the campaign even exists. Press releases can be a great way to communicate (using a standard format) with journalists and editors. There are plenty of templates for these on the web, along with advice on the best format to use for the content.

If you really struggle to write this kind of content then it might be worth considering a paid service provider. These can vary greatly in terms of both the quality and turnaround time. One site minivation uses with their clients regularly is People Per Hour (www.peopleperhour. com). Content providers on this site can be checked as other previous users leave feedback. You can also ask them questions before you commit to using them. People Per Hour also holds your payments in an escrow account which has to be released to the provider once you are happy with the service they have given you.[33]

One of the regular questions we get asked at minivation is: "Where should press releases get posted once they are written?" There is no one definitive answer to this question. Some people argue that a press release should always be sent to a paid-for news wire provider where it will be distributed to tens of thousands of journalists, others that they should always be sent to free news wire sites.

A more balanced way to approach this problem is to apply a hybrid method whereby the press release is posted to a news wire site and at the same time sent directly to individual journalists and editors with a more personalized covering email.

In reality, the media is a strategic partner to any crowdfunding project. For this reason, you need to develop and nurture a good relationship with journalists and keep them interested in your project.

A sound strategy is to draw up a list of the most influential journalists and editors in your field. Start with the following questions:

- Who are the most regular writers about topics related to your field?
- Are the writers freelance or staff?
- Who are their editors?
- Which publications do they write for?
- How frequently do they write about these topics?
- Who are the audiences for these publications?

Once you have answered these questions you will have a very deep knowledge of who they are and the journalists (and their editors) to whom you should be reaching out with your press releases. By also providing the press releases on the wider newswire service providers (free and paid for) you are more likely to attract interest from a much broader section of the media.

Broadly speaking, campaign managers need to identify the 100 most influential writers in the field. Once these people have been identified, they can then be broken down to the 10 most influential or prolific writers. By 'influential' we are also referring to their social proof (the number of followers, likes and pluses they get from their social media activities) or the interactions they are creating in their online networks.

TASK 30: TOP 100

MAKE A LIST OF 100 WRITERS IN ALL MEDIA IN YOUR FIELD.

IDENTIFY THE TOP 10 MOST INFLUENTIAL.

IDENTIFY THE TOP 10 MOST PROLIFIC.

FINALLY COMPOSE A LIST OF THE TOP WRITERS (MAXIMUM 20 PEOPLE).

VIDEO

Every campaign in all models (with the exception of interest) needs to tell its story through video. With the price of production falling and the cost of getting the video distributed now free (think Vimeo or YouTube), it starts to make a lot of sense to incorporate video into the overall message strategy.

The big question then becomes: how?

Do you take the plunge and go for it in-house or find someone who can help you create a more polished version of the story you are trying to tell? This really depends on your campaign and, of course, your budget.

In terms of the campaign, it makes sense to produce a well-polished video if, for example, you are introducing a radical new design of drinking vessel. But if you are raising money for a social cause of interest only to your local community then a really well-produced and sleek video is not necessary. A simple recording on a hand-held video camera would be sufficient to get the message across and convey the essence of the benefits to the local community.

Outsourcing the video production is great - if you can afford it!

Most production companies will want payment for their efforts once the filming and editing is completed. So make sure you get a quote for the work and have a budget that will accommodate this. Video should be thought of as an asset for the campaign. If the story in the video is told right then there should be little reason why the video could not be used again in other areas to promote the campaign.

At minivation, we recommend our clients make and produce two versions at the same time; one for the crowdfunding campaign and another more general introduction to the story for general promotional use.

Whichever route is decided upon (in-house or out-sourced production) there must be a clear reason for the video and a clear scripted message that is conveyed. When planning the video, do not just think about the words, but also the location or setting of where the story will be told, and the image on screen that the viewer will see. Using something like table 3.6.2 will provide a clear set of details about the content needed.

TABLE 3.6.2: VIDEO PRODUCTION CONTENT.

SCENE	VISUAL	VOX	NOTES

Scene is the first of the boxes above and this is the sequence you want things to appear on film. Label the sequence logically (1, 2, 3).

Visual is what we see on the video so, for example, scene one might be outside an office and the person talking to the video might be entering that office. This is exactly what would be written in the first box. The detail of what action will be seen in the end production.

Vox is the script – what does the person watching the video hear? If you have a shot of an office, for example, do you have a person talking in the background? Music? Lots of people talking at the same time (like in a busy office)? Or is the person walking into the office talking to the camera?

Finally, the *notes* section is where any relevant additional information can be given. If you are outsourcing the video production, it is still a good idea to do this exercise as it will give the video production crew a much greater understanding of the requirements of the video.

Outsourcing the production could be more cost-effective if the video crew is producing two versions at the same time. If the production team has to produce one video for the campaign and another more general production for the product or service, this is normally quite cost-effective as the crew does not need to travel and set up twice for the shooting. But obviously check this. Also ensure that two video production schedules have been completed, one for each video.

The more radical the difference between the videos, the more likely it is that costs will rise. Keeping the video as low tech as possible will ensure that costs are lower and the message becomes the centre of the video production – not the special effects used. Try to capture the heart of the campaign by filming someone, or a group of people, who will be positively impacted by the crowd's consent being given.

Many platforms require you to post the video to YouTube and then link it to the campaign's page. This means you will need a Google account if you do not already have one. The benefits of using YouTube lie in its simplicity and the breadth of the potential audience that can be reached. Uploading and then sharing video productions through this channel is really very straightforward. Instructions and help are also offered on the site, but if you are really struggling, seek assistance. It is so ubiquitous that many people in your network will surely be able to help.

Another option for the production is to see if there is any possibility of using an amateur crew to provide your video needs. Most colleges and universities have either whole classes specializing in film production or at least a society or club that is interested in this area.

These people often need experience with real-life projects to help them with their coursework or progress with their skills. You help them by providing a setting for this work and they get the experience they need. But there may also be problems in that they lack real-world experience. This may result in inappropriate music being played in the background or an essential part of the vox being edited out leaving the production with no clear message. To avoid these pitfalls be clear about what you want to say and how you want to say it through the video.

To recap, when planning your production start by thinking through the following and make sure the campaign team and the production crew are all clear about these elements of the video and why they are important:

- Make sure the video 'message' is clearly understood by all
- The message should also include a call to action for the viewer
- Demonstrate the impact this campaign will have
- Think about the viewer; try to engage with their needs and the benefits you offer
- Think about how this video will be promoted and distributed
- Include links to the video in all press releases and other promotional content
- Video is a tool where the message must be cohesive across all channels
- Think about timescales and who will produce the video

TASK 31: VIDEO PLANNING

USING THE ABOVE CRITERIA START PLANNING YOUR VIDEO.

MAKE SURE YOU HAVE ADDRESSED ALL THE ABOVE POINTS
IN THE PLAN.

UPDATES

With the rise and rise of crowdfunding, most funders understand
the need for updates and expect the campaign management to add
fresh content on a regular basis. These updates are much more than a
way for you simply to tell the network what progress you are making
behind the scenes. It is also a really powerful way for you to express
some of the hidden stories in the campaign (see section 2.9 on social
media, p168) and also to log the story as it unfolds.

This is really important because the campaign itself is now a part
of the story of the project. If, in years to come, this journey needs
describing, you have a record of this section and how the progress
was reported.

On one axis of figure 2.5.2 (p150) was trust, and on the other was
message. Updates can serve both these aspects; they add trust
because you are visibly making incremental progress towards the
end vision and they can add a level of clarity to the message as things
are explained and the reasoning behind certain decisions is made
transparent. They can also serve to reinforce the perception of the
funders that you are a credible team that can achieve the aims and
objectives you have set out to achieve.

Updates also serve as a kind of 'breaking news' feed whereby funders
are given a reason to broadcast to their network about the campaign.
News in the popular media dies away quite quickly and rarely are

stories told more than once – that is unless something new and intriguing has happened, in which case news reports can now update the public about these fresh events. It is exactly the same principle at work with your updates. No one wants to broadcast the updates that were made a week ago; however actual updates with fresh news about the campaign can be a trigger for these funders to spread the word again and again.

This same principle also provides a kind of excuse for the funder to keep coming back to the campaign without feeling like they are stalking the thing. Updates are normally emailed to the followers by the platforms themselves, but in the meantime, funders often check in from time-to-time to see what progress or changes have been made. This behaviour is perfectly normal in crowdfunding and should be encouraged by the campaign's management. Each time a funder checks in with the campaign, the chances of them broadcasting to their network about the campaign increases.

It is also true to say that the more activity your campaign can muster, the more likely you are to gain a higher profile on the platform. Platforms are self-interested in promoting their services to as wide an audience as they can reach. By turning the spotlight on campaigns that are generating a lot of buzz, they can be seen in a more positive light by this wider audience – so they encourage campaign management to update regularly and share the campaign with a wide audience. This all helps to promote the campaign and should therefore be embraced.

In terms of frequency, most platforms recommend an update every couple of days, if not daily. But be aware that some platforms will send out emailed updates together if they are added to the campaign page within a certain time frame (normally about 12 hours). This is not necessarily a problem, but it is something that should be planned before you start updating the campaign pages.

To give an example, imagine that campaign 'A' updates at 1pm on a Monday. If the management then makes a second update before 1am on Tuesday, both updates will be sent to email addresses together. So the funders get two updates in one email. It might be better to wait until after 1am on Tuesday to send the second update; perhaps at 9am on the Tuesday.

As with all aspects of a crowdfunding campaign, this is really about balance. Send too many updates and the funders may feel apathy toward the campaign, too few updates and they lose interest because progress is too slow or they lose confidence in the campaign's management. Getting this balance right will be based on the research you have done and the target users you have identified. This information should have indicated to you the channels of communication these targets prefer, and the frequency. As a minimum, minivation recommends at least one update every three days.

TASK 32: UPDATES

BASED ON YOUR RESEARCH:

WHAT CHANNELS WILL YOU USE TO UPDATE THE CROWD ABOUT YOUR CAMPAIGN?

HOW FREQUENTLY WILL THESE UPDATES HAPPEN?

WHICH TEAM MEMBER(S) WILL CREATE THESE UPDATES?

WILL THERE BE A SECOND PERSON REVIEWING OR MODERATING THE UPDATES? WHO? WHEN?

BASIC SOCIAL MEDIA

To a large extent, social media was covered in section 2.9 (p168). Here we provide a more basic introduction to the concept of trans-channel storytelling.

What we mean by trans-channel is the option to broadcast to your crowd through an almost unlimited number of channels at one time. A channel could be Facebook, a blog, a newsfeed, micro-blog service (e.g. Twitter), image-sharing facility (e.g. Pinterest) – in fact any method for getting connected with your crowd.

The general rule we follow with any channel is that only 10% of your followers will engage with your campaign and, of these 10%, only 1% is likely to provide essential crowdconsent. What needs vital consideration is the appropriateness of each channel.

This requires research. You do not want to be spending time updating a blog site, for example, when the wrong type of demographic is using this channel. Likewise, you do not want to have all your eggs in one basket. Spread the word through different channels but make sure they have a good broad-ranged audience, including your target audience you identified earlier in your research (see section 2, p104).

Generally speaking, the 10% rule applies across channels. Even then, the absolute number of people following you or 'liking' you is only half the story. For example, if you have 25,000 Twitter followers but your retweet rate and 'favourite' rate is very low, this would indicate that although people are willing to follow you, they are not really interacting with you. This is a really important point because the interactions you have with these people are what produces a wider interaction and adds weight to you and the team as *'experts'* in your field.

Your strategy in this scenario is only half working. It needs help to get those interactions started. It could mean the quality of your content needs to be improved in order to increase this interaction rate.

FINAL WORD ON CHANNELS

There are many social media platforms to consider. This is something that should be thought through early in the planning stages. Also set out from the beginning the rules of engagement for your campaign.

For example, most of the campaigns minivation works on have a '*no personal information*' rule. This means no personal information is given in any of the updates. It helps keep the dialogue on a professional level and removes any criticism being aimed at personal issues or tastes. It makes it more objective.

The best place to find further help is online. If you are new to a platform such as LinkedIn, for example, ask existing users for guidance about the best way to navigate the site. It's amazing how many wonderful people are out there who are willing to help newbies to these sites. Alternatively, of course, there are plenty of helpful blogs and videos that will also guide you on best practice.

Get started early and test everything. If you pre-crowdfund you can get much deeper feedback on these aspects and fine tune your social media use while also building a small following before going live.

TASK 33: CHANNEL FIT

CHOOSE THE SOCIAL MEDIA CHANNELS MOST APPROPRIATE TO YOUR CAMPAIGN.

NOW JUSTIFY THE CHOICES WITH HARD RESEARCH.

FOR EXAMPLE, IF YOU DECIDE TO USE TWITTER, SHOW WHY THIS FITS WITH YOUR CAMPAIGN.

NOW REPEAT FOR ALL CHANNELS.

3.7

ACTIVE SENTENCES

Compare these two sentences:

1. minivation creates crowdfunding campaigns
2. Crowdfunding campaigns are created by people

Answer these questions:

- In which of the above are we interested in the team that does the action?
- In which sentence are we only interested in the action?
- In the second sentence do you know who creates campaigns?
- Which sentence did you prefer?

If you said sentence one, then you preferred the active sentence. Sentence two was using the passive form. Using the passive is not incorrect, there are times when the passive is actually more appropriate than the active form. However when it comes to writing a pitch then, as a general rule, the active form trumps the passive.

This is because your pitch needs to motivate the crowd to action!

With an active sentence (example sentence one) the reader can understand who (the subject) is doing the action. It also helps to clarify what action is required of the reader. This is sometimes called the 'imperative' and it functions just like an active sentence, but with a bit more zest. We like to think of them as commands from the pitch to the reader. It is asking the reader to perform some action or another.

Look at these parts of sentences:

A) Fund us and you will receive…
B) You can get it by pledging…
C) Pledgers will get…
D) By helping this campaign…
E) This project hopes to get funded by…
F) These items will be shipped in June 2018…

How did you feel when you were reading the above? Most people will feel slightly less motivated by D), E) and F) than by A), B) and C). Even though there is no clear action/value being described in any of the above examples the wording of the first three moves people more than the last three. There is a feeling of urgency to them.

Language is a really important part of the pitch and one that needs careful attention. In section 1.5 (p75), we met the two US academics Tanushree Mitra and Eric Gilbert who, in their 2014 conference paper (from Computer and Supported Co-operative Work, Baltimore), detailed a study they had done on the language used in both successful and unsuccessful US campaigns with Kickstarter.

Some of the more successful phrases included:

PROJECT WILL BE	DIFFERENCE FOR
HAS PLEDGED	PLEDGED WILL
PLEDGED AND	GIVEN THE CHANCE
WE CAN AFFORD	YOUR CONTINUED
USED IN A	THEIR CREATIVE
MENTION YOU	TO BUILD THIS
OPTION IS	INSPIRED ME
WORKSHOP AND	PROJECT WILL ALLOW
THE COMING	ACCESSIBLE TO THE
WE HAVE CHOSEN	FROM THE PAST
AND AN INVITE	FINDING OUT
ALL SUPPORTERS	PLUS RECOGNITION
PLEDGERS WILL	GOT YOU
WANT THEM TO	SECURE THE
AND ENCOURAGEMENT	SOME HELP WITH
THAT EXISTS	AS PEOPLE
IN THIS NEW	PROJECTS WILL
WOULD GREATLY	WE ARE FULLY
DATES AND	A NATIONAL
CONCEPTION	PROBLEM OF
AND ADDED	KIND TO
UNVEILING	GOOD KARMA AND
COMMEMORATING THE	SHOWS THAT
GIRL AND	A PERSONAL TOUR
TWO FRIENDS	THE MEANING
FUTURE IS	THEIR THOUGHTS
THAT I FEEL	SUPPORT AT
FUNDRAISING GOAL	ARE RAISING MONEY
ALSO RECEIVE TWO	GOOD AS

UPFRONT	AND DEVELOP
LOOKING FOR YOU	THE INSIDE OF
FOR TWO YEARS	TO PLAY THE
GAIN A	AS A SMALL
ANSWERING	CHANGED MY
FUNDING WILL HELP	OUR SOCIAL
COMPANY FOR	DESIGN ELEMENTS
THANKS A	GUARANTEE A
SHARING WITH	ALL PREVIOUS REWARDS
MESSAGE AND	A DETAILED
POSTER OF YOUR	THE CORRECT
A LOT ABOUT	AND SHARE IT

TABLE 3.7.1: SAMPLE KEY SUCCESS PHRASES - ADAPTED FROM MITRA AND GILBERT (2014)[22]

This list is by no means exhaustive, but it is remarkable how many of these phrases (and others) we have witnessed being used with varying degrees of success. No one phrase can guarantee a campaign's success. It is a combination of using the words in the right context that will get you results in crowdfunding. To provide some sort of balance to this section we want to also include the attention words by Carol Bentley.[34] But we have changed a few to better fit a crowdfunding campaign with useful key words:

FREE	READY	REMARKABLE
BARGAIN	SECRETS	POWERFUL
NOW	NEVER BEFORE	OFFER
IMPROVED	IT'S HERE	MAGIC
INTRODUCING	NEW	INCREDIBLE
JUST ARRIVED	AMAZING	HERE/ HERE IS

SAVE	WIN	GREATEST
BREAK THROUGH	LAST CHANCE	COMPARE
PLEDGE NOW	ANNOUNCING	CHALLENGE
BONUS	GUARANTEED	BARGAIN
GIFT	DISCOUNT	ADVICE
VALUABLE	FIRST TIME EVER	THESE
PRIORITY	SPECIAL	LOVE
UNIQUE	INSTANTLY	PHENOMENAL
RUSH	DISCOVER	REVEALING
THE TRUTH ABOUT	FOREVER	SUCCESSFUL
YOU(R)	PREMIUM	ASTONISHING
ONLY THIS CAMPAIGN	WHY	EXCITING
EASY	WHO ELSE	EXCLUSIVE
HURRY	WHICH	FANTASTIC
TODAY	WANTED	FASCINATING
HOW TO	THIS	INITIAL
AT LAST	SUDDENLY	SUPER
LIMITED	STARTLING	TIME-SENSITIVE
OPPORTUNITY	SENSATIONAL	URGENT
POSITIVE IMPACT	QUICK	MIRACLE
WONDERFUL	REVOLUTIONARY	PLEDGE

**TABLE 3.7.2: ATTENTION WORDS FOR ANY PITCH -
ADAPTED FROM BENTLEY (2005)[34]**

These words are useful to have to hand when writing your pitch. A good sprinkling of these can really help your writing. As with everything in life though, balance is the key. Too many of these words and phrases and you might end up with a jumbled mess that grammatically makes sense but is much less appealing than it should be.

A great tip is to record yourself saying the pitch before you start to write. Imagine you are with friends, you feel relaxed in their company. Now tell them about the campaign and the benefits it offers. By doing this with an imaginary audience, members of which you like and with whom you feel comfortable, you will use phrases and words that convey the essence of the pitch in simple terms. In other words, you will tend to get to the point more directly rather than going around the houses searching for words and phrases to use.

Use this recording as the transcript for the writing of the pitch. You may want to add some things and take other things out, but at least you will have a good guide to help you create that all important written pitch.

TASK 34: RECORDING YOUR PITCH

RECORD YOUR PITCH.

THEN WRITE IT UP AND PRE-CROWDFUND IT.

ASK FAMILY, FRIENDS AND COLLEAGUES TO COMMENT, VOTE AND SPREAD THE WORD.

THIS WILL BE A GOOD INDICATION OF HOW SUCCESSFUL THE CAMPAIGN WILL BE.

3.8

THE MEDIA OUTPOURING

Section 2.9 dealt in more detail with the social media aspects of any campaign and ground rules were introduced in sections 2.4 and 3.6. So in this section, we are going to concentrate more on the actual content you need to be distributing through these channels.

Ground rules are worth repeating because they need to be established for each communication channel early in the planning stages. The golden rule is stick to them as much as you can, but if you need to ignore them ensure you can justify this action to your team.

Ground rules are established for a very simple reason; they provide the glue for your communications. There are many great books out there on branding and communication but one thing that many people forget to mention is that the early ground rules must be set out clearly and adhered to. They can change later once the campaign is over and they can be re-written or changed to better accommodate the new position of the vision you have created. But while the campaign is live, stick to them as far as possible.

We are labouring this point on purpose. It needs to be understood and used as a guiding principle by all members of the team. This also extends beyond the immediate communications through the campaign channels and to the personal updates on Facebook and the like.

The reason for this extension is that people will associate your opinions with those of the campaign even when you are writing a personal statement about something on your self-branded channel (blog, Twitter, Facebook and so on). Just look at how many academics or professionals feel compelled to state that the "opinions expressed here are not those of Brand XYZ" or "all opinions expressed here are my own"; even so, people can make associations with the expressions being put forward in a personal space and the organization for or with which that person works.

For this reason, care and attention must be taken and the ground rules followed. Some classic ground rules are:

- No online communications after consumption of alcohol
- No talk about private lives on campaign communications
- No negative comments about competitors or funders
- Always use at least one attention word
- If something upsets you, take a break before responding (at least one hour)
- Online correspondence only happens between 7am and 7pm – local time
- Be sensitive to the campaign, while it is live, at all times

Some of these are fairly straightforward and perhaps a little obvious. They can be adjusted to suit your needs but they may help to provide some inspiration for you and the team writing for you.

It may seem paradoxical that we stated earlier to stick with these at all times but there should also be a degree of flexibility. For example, no talking about private lives is fine unless something has happened that relates to the campaign in a positive way.

Imagine that one of your team is in a restaurant and another customer in that restaurant is a funder and speaks highly about the campaign to your team member. Of course you would want to tell the world about this. This is fantastic news and will certainly help to send a quality signal out to the wider community.

This is a very positive scenario but if it were reversed and the team member was actually in the middle of an argument with the fellow customer this would need to be dealt with quickly.

News, whether positive or negative, can go viral among the community quite quickly!

If negative news does get out, make sure you deal with it fast and respond to everyone you can. Time is of the essence in this scenario. The news story will die down and be put to rest soon enough, but by being seen to be proactive you are once again shifting the negative to a more positive light. Never revisit this scenario in the future unless absolutely essential to do so. News, once dead, will not resurface unless something new triggers it.

For example, if you blog towards the end of the campaign about what a turbulent time this has been, the negatives will start to resurface and someone who did not have the chance to make a detrimental comment at the time of the original turbulence may feel they can now express their opinion. Once again, this problem, that had gone away, will resurface and needs precious time and attention to be dealt with.

These are extreme scenarios but thinking about them can help you gauge the kind of responses that are appropriate to some circumstances. Role-playing this kind of thing can also help strengthen your team and provide you with an insight into their strengths and weaknesses.

On a more positive note, the media outpouring can also be a very lifting experience giving the team members an opportunity to express their creativity in all sorts of ways. Updates are just one element of this outpouring; video, press releases, photos, illustrations, graphics and even music has been, and can be, used to help get the message across.

No matter which channel is used, or the content the message, it must be consistent. It should always reinforce the main aims and objectives of the campaign and, ultimately, the vision being created. By doing so, the campaign is more likely to trigger crowdconsent.

TASK 35: CRITICISM

WHO STANDS TO LOSE OUT WITH THE INTRODUCTION OF YOUR CAMPAIGN?

OUTLINE THE OPPOSITION S ARGUMENT TO THE CAMPAIGN.

HOW CAN THESE ARGUMENTS BE COUNTERED?

3.9

OVER TARGET

This section is only relevant to donation and reward model crowdfunding campaigns.

Section 1.2 and 3.3 both mentioned stretch goals and how they function. This section goes into a little more detail about the need to have a plan for going over target. All money raised through crowdfunding must be accounted for. Transparency is the key in this concept and the greatest transparency is needed concerning money.

In section 1.1, we were introduced to the issue of moral hazard and this can be just as significant in any of the two models we look at below. It is essential to have some sort of plan to demonstrate that you have a sound idea of what impact the campaign will have if it goes over the financial targets.

The interest model is not included in this section because loans that are made in this model tend to be a Dutch auction. This means that people who make offers to lend to these companies are bidding down the interest on the loan.

For example person 'A' offers to lend £10 at 9% interest, person 'B' will offer £10 at a lower level of interest (say 8.9%) and so on. The company will only take the loan amount it is seeking (let us imagine it wants £50,000). So as more people add their money they will try to get their money loaned out at the best price, so for this reason they may choose to lend at 8.9% or lower. They want their money to be loaned out quickly so it can start earning interest. This downward pressure on the interest rate is called a Dutch auction; compare it to auctions on eBay or QuiBids and you see the opposite. People are purchasing an item of some description and so the offers for the item keep going up, not down.

For this reason, the interest model is excluded for the reasons that follow. The project only gets to take away the money it asks for, it is often restricted from going over this target.

The donation model is by far the simplest to manage. This is because the value being created tends to be something for the common good, a social cause or a community project of some description, that has a benefit beyond an individual trying to raise money for a more focused or self-centred project.

Generally, people are happy to see a good cause raising the money it needs to create the value it wants to create and thus benefit others in the process. Nevertheless, it is still a good idea to have a plan to communicate the greater impact the project will have once it goes over target.

There is also nothing wrong with broadcasting this early in the campaign's life cycle as it shows the project has ambition and can increase the positive impacts with additional income. This may, in turn, lead to a stronger motivational message being delivered to the audience leading to greater consent being granted.

A statement should also be a little restrained. Broadcasting a realistic over-target message is fine, but going over-the-top with this kind of communication could possibly have a detrimental effect. Balance is the key to getting this message across in an appropriate manner.

For the donation model, research into other campaigns and what they have done to help gain crowdconsent is vital. Campaigns that are willing to state their intentions, but within a realistic timeframe (and financial target) are often the ones reaching their goals fastest.

Depending on the sector your campaign is in, reaching target can be problematic and raising more than this is, in probability, quite unlikely to happen. But be prepared; after all, you never know what may happen with your donation model campaign.

For the reward model, stretch goals can play a vital role in the life of a campaign as they can show that you are thinking beyond the constraints of the vision you are creating. They can also help focus the crowd externally on the next step of the project. They do this by allowing the crowd to have a say, a voice, in the direction in which the project could go in.

In a way, this is crowdsourcing, where the crowd's input can add tremendous value to the project. Imagine you have developed a vessel for consuming energy drinks while on the move, but to fill it you need to remove the cap to drink, which could then be lost. An individual in the crowd could have the solution for tethering the cap to the main container.

Immediately, a new practical element is added to the project that creates added value for both the user and to the functionality of the product itself, not to mention the aesthetic appeal this may add to the end design.

So what happened in this scenario is really straightforward (with hindsight), but is actually a complex interaction. Members of the community have taken it upon themselves to create something that delivers a much more beneficial end result. In other words, they have taken it upon themselves to use their cognition to be innovative and apply their creativity to a specific problem.

For the management of the campaign, this is awesome because it not only shows a genuine love for the vision but also that you have now engaged at a much deeper level with the working customer. A massive thank you and great kudos should be extended to the individual who came up with the original idea.

This type of activity can also help internally with the team behind a campaign. When such a thing happens, it can lift the morale of a team as it provides hard evidence that the crowd is engaged with you, beyond simply adding funds.

TASK 36: MORE MONEY

WRITE A STATEMENT ON THE USE OF THE OVER TARGET MONEY AND THE LIKELY IMPACT THIS WILL HAVE ON YOUR VISION.

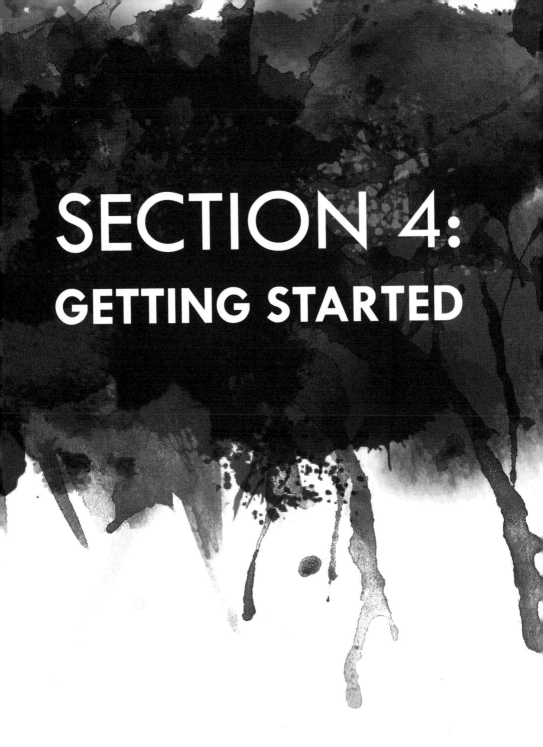

SECTION 4:
GETTING STARTED

No entity has a monopoly on crowdfunding (although several might believe they do or wish they had!). Crowdfunding is open to interpretation and it should be remembered that this is nothing new; it is only the means of communication, via the internet, that is new.

Our point here is that there are several innovative resources available and our contribution, under the Minivation brand, is this book and the free resources that can be found on the minivation.co site.

These resources provide you with a great place to start planning and thinking through your campaign; there is even an opportunity to speak with an expert directly via Skype or Google Hangout, just get in touch!

More resources will be added and we are fully aware that we do not know it all, so if you have ideas about what should be included or how to improve our existing library please get in touch via: ideas@minivation.co

Hope to speak soon.
Chris

CROWDSHED - A CASE STUDY

CROWDFUNDING PLATFORM	CrowdShed (www.crowdshed.com)
PROJECT NAME	Midnight of My Life - A short film about Steve Marriott
FUNDING TYPE	Rewards and donations
FUNDING TARGET	£12,000
AMOUNT RAISED	£15,563
NUMBER OF FUNDERS	202
PROJECT LENGTH	40 days
CROWDFUNDING PAGE	https://www.crowdshed.com/projects/midnight-of-my-life-a-new-short-film

PROJECT SYNOPSIS

Midnight Of My Life is a short film about British guitarist and musician Steve Marriott, who made his name as a solo artist and frontman of legendary sixties mod group, Small Faces.

Led by scriptwriter Nina Gerstenberger and director Phil Davis, *Midnight* will run up to 10 minutes in length and focuses on one specific moment in Marriott's career that defined his 'music first; fame and money second' attitude.

Looking to fund the film in its entirety from script to screen, the £12,000 funding target covered equipment and location hire, cast and crew salaries, post-production and licensing costs for Marriott's music.

PROJECT TEAM

Midnight was approached professionally with an established and dedicated team in place to take care of every aspect of the crowdfunding project, from launch to success. This enabled us to react quickly to enquiries and questions and keep project momentum strong right through to the end date.

The team consists of professional, experienced film producers and director, a Steve Marriott biographer, and a composer and musician. All experienced across our respective fields, we had one crucial thing in common – we were all huge fans of Steve Marriott and were motivated to make this project succeed not for money, but for a love of the subject matter.

Phil Davis explains, "I grew up loving the Small Faces. I haven't directed anything on film for 12 years, and to be honest, I wasn't planning to. But when producer Hatty Hodgson sent me the script for *Midnight Of My Life*, I changed my mind."

Producer – Hatty Hodgson
Producer – Pamela Drameh
Scriptwriter – Nina Gerstenberger
Director – Phil Davis
Consultant – John Helier
Composer – Andy Bell

WHAT TOOLS DID YOU USE TO PROMOTE YOUR CROWDFUND PROJECT?

FACEBOOK - MIDNIGHT OF MY LIFE PAGE

WWW.FACEBOOK.COM/MIDNIGHTOFMYLIFE

989 likes at end of campaign
500+ likes prior to launch
42 posts during the 40-day campaign
Page created two weeks before campaign go-live date

One week prior to launch, we posted one 'meet the team' story each day, introducing the key players behind the film and the crowdfund project and inviting their followers and networks to get involved. This is a great way to 'personalize' the project and give the crowd real insight into who is behind it and why – an important factor in any crowdfund.

TWITTER – @STEVESHORTFILM

HTTPS://TWITTER.COM/STEVESHORTFILM

451 followers
46 tweets during the 40-day campaign
Page created two weeks before campaign go-live date
Hashtags used (in order of priority):
#SteveMarriott
#MidnightOfMyLife
#SmallFaces

YOUTUBE – MIDNIGHT OF MY LIFE VIDEO

HTTPS://WWW.YOUTUBE.COM/WATCH?V=XDY2YRMOFDW&FEATURE=YOUTU.BE

54 views

BLOG – LEND US A QUID

HTTPS://WWW.CROWDSHED.COM/BLOG/LEND-US-A-QUID

Midnight scriptwriter Nina Gerstenberger penned a guest article for the CrowdShed blog, which CrowdShed and the *Midnight* team then circulated to their networks and on to a wider audience, raising awareness of the film and the motivation behind it.

This blog struck a chord and was circulated globally, inspiring a late flurry of funding from the mod community in Japan (bizarrely and surprisingly) which ultimately led to *Midnight* hitting its target and entering a period of overfunding.

EVENT – MEET THE FILMMAKERS!

HTTP://WWW.EVENTBRITE.CO.UK/E/MIDNIGHT-OF-MY-LIFE-MEET-THE-FILMMAKERS-TICKETS-14750762929

39 attendees
Free entry
Speakers included Phil Davis (director), Pamela Drameh (producer), and Paulo Hewitt and John Hellier (Marriott biographers)

The filmmaker team behind *Midnight* held an evening event at The Shed, the CrowdShed event space open to use for free to anyone crowdfunding on the platform. We set aside a small budget for drinks and snacks.

The format was a two-hour event introducing the key players in the crowdfund project with a series of short presentations and stories from Marriott's lively life, followed by a Q&A with the audience.
Music was curated by project composer Andy Bell (Oasis, Beady Eye).

Drinks flowed and the stories of Marriott's wild escapades grew ever wilder as told by friends, fans and biographers. It's safe to say that it's been a long time since central London had hosted so many dedicated mods (hairstyles and all) in one place so successfully.

GRAPH ILLUSTRATING PAGE VIEWS FOR *MIDNIGHT OF MY LIFE* **ON CROWDSHED.COM**

DIGGING DEEPER

Some basic data analysis reveals some interesting insight into the success of *Midnight*'s aggressive social media campaigning.

During the course of the project, Midnight received 8,777 page views. This accounted for 17% of all traffic to crowdshed.com in that period, equating to a page view rate 77% higher than any other project. A powerful indicator of the value of visibility and market penetration.

Of these circa 9,000 visits, 69% were referrals from other websites, by far the most important and valuable of which was Facebook (half of all referrals), driven by regular social updates and stories from CrowdShed and the team behind *Midnight*.

Modern data crunching also gave us invaluable information on popular times to fund, both by day and hour. This helped focus communications, tailor them to days and times and work out when something we said was most likely to create a reaction, or crucially, a donation.

With *Midnight*, 50% of all traffic came over the weekends and peak

DAY / HOUR	00/01	02/03	04/05	06/07	08/09	10/11	12/13	14/15	16/17	18/19	20/21	22/23
Monday	36	11	10	32	62	76	82	107	144	135	128	73
Tuesday	26	7	11	32	57	82	113	98	111	123	113	82
Wednesday	26	9	5	33	55	81	111	99	120	98	132	65
Thursday	31	7	17	36	47	76	74	78	77	77	109	81
Friday	48	12	14	23	43	143	275	190	172	133	147	80
Saturday	62	26	11	18	76	99	99	104	129	136	119	85
Sunday	44	14	10	20	53	81	87	141	189	173	162	97

funding hours were around Friday lunch time (ah… the end of week apathy that slows down all our working practices to a crawl) and Sunday afternoon.

The heat map on page 241 shows transaction times, from dark blue representing very cold (fewest transactions) through to bright red representing peak activity.

WHAT DID YOU DO RIGHT?

We set a great foundation with our rewards. We felt it crucial to address a range of price points that appealed to everyone, from a simple £5 donation right the way through to a chance to appear in the film for £200. "Money can't buy" is an oft-used term, but we embraced it to great effect with everything from an invite to the launch party to a personalized plectrum.

We targeted influencers and celebrities active in the music industry and, in particular, mod worlds – Paul Weller, Paulo Hewitt, Andy Bell (who subsequently came on board as composer) – and used their networks to gain exposure and drum up excitement for what we were doing. Ambassadors are a great way to easily target a pre-qualified interested audience.

We built and maintained momentum. In crowdfunding we soon discovered momentum is everything and if you drop the ball for a minute you could lose a possible order. By posting regularly to our social networks, emailing funders to thank them, hosting an event and sending out newsletters and pushing for press coverage we never let the world forget about our campaign. It paid off.

MIDNIGHT BY NUMBERS

- Average time spent on the page was five minutes versus three mins 43 seconds for crowdshed.com average
- *Midnight* brought 3,862 new visitors to crowdshed.com
- A total of 637 site visits came from links shared by people using the project page web sharing tools (Facebook, Twitter and email). This represents 25% of all site traffic from web sharing
- Visits to the page generated 178 transactions at 2.72% conversion rate – a 5% increase over the average crowdshed.com conversion rate
- Average transaction value was £76 versus an average of £69 for crowdshed.com
- A total of 16% of all transactions were donations, despite rewards being available

Since the CrowdShed campaign finished, the *Midnight of My Life* team announced that Martin Freeman (star of *Sherlock*, *The Hobbit* and *The Office*) has just taken the lead role in the film. This also demonstrates another benefit of crowdfunding - project success can help to attract talent as the project has effectively been derisked or "validated" by the crowd.

KRITICALMASS CASE STUDY - POWERING GOOD

FUNDING TYPE	REWARD BASED
FUNDING TARGET	£7,000 (ORGINALLY) - THE HAVE EXTENDED AND ADDED STRETCH TARGET OF £15,000. PART OF THE KRITICALMASS PHILOSOPHY IS THAT CROWDFUNDING CAMPAIGNS CAN CREATE A MOVEMENT AND SUSTAIN A LONGER STORY ARCH
AMOUNT RAISED	£8,533 (AS OFF TODAY 06.02.2015)
NUMBER OF FUNDERS/ SUPPORTERS:	84 (AS OFF TODAY 06.02.2015)
PROJECT LENGTH	96 DAYS
CROWDFUNDING PAGE	HTTPS://KRITICALMASS.COM/P/ ALEM2RIO2016

The core principle behind kriticalmass.com is to enable inspiring people and ideas not only to get the funds they need but to build a community of skilled volunteers, mentors, promoters and corporate partners that ensure a lasting legacy. Crowdfunding can, and should, be much more than just a way of accessing funds or a new sales channel. Crowdfunding has the incredible ability to allow people from across the globe to become part of an authentic story and inspired community. And rarely do we come across a story as inspiring, uplifting and worthy of the crowd's support as that of Alem Mumuni.

MEET ALEM

Alem Mumuni, three times African Paracycling champion, was born into a peasant family in rural Ghana. Alem lost the use of his right leg due to poliomyelitis at the age of two. In a country where 7-10% of the population is physically disabled and face incredible discrimination, Alem fought back, crawling for nine years of his life until he eventually learned to walk with the aid of a wooden stick.

These hardships did not manage to break Alem's spirit or athletic drive. He first encountered cycling through necessity, riding to help speed up his long daily journey to school. Fast-forward to 2012 and Alem became the first Ghanaian athlete ever to qualify for the Paralympics without a wild card entry. Ranked second in the world for his C2 class and with a great shot at a medal, Alem's dreams were cruelly shattered. And just a week before his time trial he contracted chicken pox from within the Olympic village, making it impossible to compete at his world-class standard.

GETTING BEHIND A COMEBACK KID

It speaks to Alem's character how quickly he recovered from this blow, immediately turning his focus to Rio 2016. Alem's main motivation and drive is not only to win the first Paralympic medal for Ghana, but also to change the country's perception towards people with physical disabilities. Unlike top athletes in the US or UK, he receives very limited funds from the Ghanaian Paralympics Committee, making it extremely challenging to train for, and travel to, qualifying competitions around the world. Alem turned to the crowd through his campaign on kriticalmass to get a fighting chance at fulfilling his dream.

A TEAM OF SKILLS

A solid starting point for Alem's successful crowdfunding campaign was his realization that he could not go it alone. Statistics show that crowdfunding teams are more successful than individual crowdfunders. And while having more hands on board is obviously helpful, realizing what you lack and attracting the right skill-set to your team has the biggest impact. Having Alex Main, a 23-year-old sports science graduate from Devon, volunteer to coach Alem and create a training plan for Rio 2016, was a major breakthrough. Equally, London-based senior funding specialist Alistair Lamond volunteered to help Alem with the day-to-day running of his crowdfunding campaign.

EVEN A GREAT STORY REQUIRES HARD HARD WORK

All too often, we witness project creators who seem to believe in the "if I build it they will come" mantra, hoping for magic virality and instant approval. The truth is that successful campaigns are not just built on great ideas and clear targets but on hard work. Unfortunately, there are no short-cuts, even though frequent media coverage of overnight crowdfunding successes would make you believe otherwise. Crafting a great story, video and rewards are very important, but without the right communications push nobody will get to see your hard work. Despite having full-time jobs and rigorous training schedules, the team around Alem realized the challenge ahead early and shifted into highest gear.

IDENTIFYING YOUR TARGETS

Like any marketing campaign, it is crucial to understand the appeal for your specific audiences.

Alem's project has universal appeal; it's the story of an underdog, and it's a tale of persistence, hope and beating the odds. It is the stuff of Hollywood movies or Nike commercials. Capturing the appeal of your story in the imagery and copy you use is essential in driving engagement. And as with most stories, in Alem's case, there were angles to the story that allowed for even more focused targeting. After targeting friends and existing supporters, the team focused on engaging with the Ghanaian Diaspora and the paracycling community.

ENGAGING THOSE IN THE CROWD THAT MATTER MOST

The crowd is not equal. There are some members who have a decisively larger network and a louder voice; the influencers. Social media channels and tools make it easier than ever to identify and approach them. Using LinkedIn, Twitter and Facebook as well as tools such as Followerwonk, the team managed to engage which people they knew were not only incredibly receptive to the message but could effectively promote the story. In fact, the first backer, beyond friends and families, was Sophie Christiansen a five-time gold medal winning Paralympic equestrian. The team simply tweeted a link to the kritialmass project page and asked her to support a fellow Paralympics athlete. Not only did she share the page and donate money, she also agreed to create a video support message. Another outcome of this strategy was a player of the Ghanaian national football team donating flights to qualifying events in the US.

ACTIVATING EXISTING COMMUNITIES

Building a new community is hard work; activating an existing and aligned community can be a lot more effective. Being aware of Rotary's 'End Polio Now' initiative, kriticalmass approached Devin Thorpe, a journalist who is part of the Rotary network and who had previously covered kriticalmass. Devin not only featured the story on Forbes.com but also introduced Alem to the global Rotary network. The result? He was featured on Rotary's website and invited to speak at Rotary events and fundraisers.

HARNESSING THE CREATIVITY AND INTELLIGENCE OF THE CROWD

While it is easy to focus on their wallets, your crowd has a lot more to give. Besides straightforward promotion members may have helpful skills and ideas. In Alem's case, we asked the kriticalmass community, our friends at One-Minute Briefs and leading creative schools (e.g. Sweden's Hyper Island) to create a print ad that would tell Alem's story. Not only did the hundreds of entries do this in unique and surprising ways but the students pushing out the work to their networks was a great booster. Thanks to this different approach and creative output, the winning ad was featured in the *Metro UK* and shown to more than 3 million people.

CREATING A LEGACY THROUGH THE CROWD

Through a unique and inspiring story, the right team, hard work and a focused push-out campaign the project did not only reach the funds necessary to get Alem to the qualifying events but managed to build a community of skilled and passionate supporters who now back Alem in his dream of shifting the perceptions of disabilities in Ghana. And hopefully his supporters will get to feel like they played a part in winning gold in Rio.

COCOON COMPLETE HOME SECURITY CASE STUDY: CROWDFUNDING AS THE FIRST STEP IN BUILDING A SUCCESSFUL PRODUCT AND SUSTAINABLE BUSINESS.

FUNDING TYPE	PERKS BASED
FUNDING TARGET	100,000 USD, NOW IN INDEMAND, OUR NEW SERVICE THAT ENABLES CAMPAIGN OWNERS TO SEAMLESSLY TRANSITION INTO THE NEXT PHASE OF OPERATIONS, INCLUDING ACCEPTING PRODUCT PRE-ORDERS, CUSTOMER ACQUISITION AND EARNINGS GROWTH. WE ARE COMMITTED TO HELPING OUR ENTREPRENEURS AS MUCH AS POSSIBLE. BEING ABLE TO FOCUS ON PRODUCTION WHILST STILL TAKING PRE-ORDERS ON THEIR INDIEGOGO PAGE, WHICH HAS HIGH SEO AND PR DRIVEN TRAFFIC, WAS SOMETHING OUR CUSTOMERS ASKED FOR.
AMOUNT RAISED	221,178 USD ON INDIEGOGO (AS OF TODAY 27.03.2015) PLUS A 1M INVESTMENT ROUND OUTSIDE OF INDIEGOGO IN LESS THAN 1 YEAR.
NUMBER OF FUNDERS/ SUPPORTERS:	788 (AS OFF TODAY 27.03.2015)
PROJECT LENGTH	37 DAY CAMPAIGN, NOW IN INDEMAND
CROWDFUNDING PAGE	WWW.INDIEGOGO.COM/PROJECTS/COCOON-COMPLETE-HOME-SECURITY-FROM-ONE-DEVICE

OUR MISSION

Indiegogo was founded to democratize access to capital. Our founders, Danae Ringelmann, Slava Rubin and Eric Schell had each faced challenges with raising finance, and they couldn't understand why there wasn't a better way. So many people are locked out of traditional finance and therefore many ideas that the world would have benefited from, were not coming to life. They decided to change this and started Indiegogo in 2008, the world's first and now largest global crowdfunding platform. We have seen over 300,000 campaigns from 224 countries and territories and we distribute millions of dollars all across the world each week.

Our mission is to empower anyone, anywhere, to fund what matters to them, whether it is entrepreneurial, a creative project or a great cause.

Technology is an incredibly interesting area. Over the past few years we have seen Indiegogo become an incubation platform for innovative ideas and new technologies. Crowfunding is not just about the money, there is huge value in the crowd and the best campaigns harness this.

We believe that crowdfunding is a crucial step in building not only a successful product, but a sustainable business. It's so important to validate your idea and gain feedback from your users before you launch to market. Startups and large companies are now making products that people actually want rather than products they think the market wants. Aside from the valuable insight into product-market fit, running an Indiegogo campaign also enables you capture data against your customers, figure out new customer segments and even entire markets - Sensibo is a small Israeli company and through their campaign they realised they had a strong market in Singapore. As a result, they now have a distributor in that region. Misfit Shine had funders from 85 countries and realised from the start that they needed a strong international marketing strategy; they still sell more product outside the US than within the US.

Most interestingly running a great crowdfunding campaign opens up doors to retailers, distributors and further funding. Physical products and hardware need a lot of capital to produce and scale and traditionally investors were hesitant to invest in a product that has not yet proved market potential.

Crowdfunding enables you to de-risk your product and raise further finance. We are seeing VC investment into Indiegogo campaign every few weeks now, with the most recent being Skully, Motorcycle AR helmet raising $11m 2 weeks ago and Jibo the family robot raising $25M last month. Since 2013 successful Indiegogo campaigns have raised a combined $210 million in follow-on venture funding. Crowdfunding platforms like Indiegogo are helping to develop the hardware investment landscape and de-risk investment into innovative products.

INTRODUCING COCOON

In early 2014 our founding team found that their traditional home security systems kept giving off false alarms and in doing so reap misery on their neighbours. This meant that the team soon found that they would only occasionally set the expensive professionally installed alarm systems, making them useless and leaving their homes unprotected.

Home security systems hadn't evolved much in the last 20 years and weren't really accessible for most people (e.g. new home owners / tenants) due to cost and complexity of installation. After removing the offending devices (with very little grace) our experienced team came together to build a smart home device that is simple to use, accessible to anyone and beautifully designed.

Our vision, to create a device that is so simple anyone could use it, that is so easy to install you can do it yourself in seconds, and that is smart enough to eliminate false alarms. This meant that we needed to be able to sense activity outside of the room, through walls and doors.

The solution is Cocoon, a smart-device that makes home security simple and accessible. A single Cocoon can protect your whole home, learning what's normal to avoid false alarms and make securing your home effortless.

Cocoon was co-founded by five British serial entrepreneurs with a number of successful exits behind them. Dan Conlon started his first business, Donhost, while at high school and sold it for in 2005, later founding cloud sync & storage service Humyo, which to Trend Micro in 2010. Sanjay Parekh was CEO of Webexpenses, which sold in 2012, and together with Colin Richardson, Nick Gregory and John Berthels they founded Cocoon.

A NEW WAY OF SOLVING AN OLD PROBLEM

We set ourselves the challenge of being able to protect a whole home from just one device. The home security products in the market today are too complicated and expensive.

The breakthrough came when we realised that we could measure infrasound (sound below 20Hz - that the human ear can't hear) and profile that data to understand if the activity is a homeowner coming home or an intruder attempting to break in.

GEARING UP

We planned well ahead of our crowdfunding launch and took seriously the advice that the Indiegogo team shared with us. We invested in growing a list of our earliest supporters ahead of launch by driving live traffic to our website (www.cocoon.life) from Facebook ads and

Google Adwords over a period of two months. The mailing list is a collection of people interested in purchasing a Cocoon as soon as we send the campaign live. We would set ourselves objectives, targets to hit, and improve aspects of our messaging and positioning to increase our conversion rates until we hit our goal of 1,800 signups.

Having a large group of early supporters meant that when we were ready to push the button and send the campaign live we could be sure to gain momentum quickly with a large amount of early sales. By planning ahead we managed to hit our crowdfunding target within the first 4 days of it going live!

WHERE IS COCOON NOW?

In less than 12 months we've raised just over £1m in seed funding from an Internet of things focused venture fund and a crowdfunding campaign that smashed its target in under 4 days selling the first Cocoons to buyers in over 50 countries.

Cocoon has expanded rapidly. From a founding team of five, with three successful exits, we've grown to a team of twenty with two offices in the UK and plans to expand into the US.
As well as winning a London Design Award, Cocoon was named by Forbes' as one of its "Five British digital businesses to watch in 2015", by The Times as one of their Top 10 UK start-ups and have been invited to Number 10 Downing Street and the Palace!

ANYONE CAN DO IT: INDIEGOGO TOP TIPS

We have over 7 years of data from the 300,000+ campaigns that have run on our platform and our team have mined that data for trends and insights into what makes a successful campaign. We have numerous resources to help you set up a great campaign and we love to share our experience and expertise to help bring as many great ideas to reality. Here are our top tips to run a successful campaign:

START BY SETTING YOUR GOALS

Think of your crowdfunding campaign as a marathon, not a sprint. I would say it's best to run a campaign for 30-45 days; it's a long enough period to raise awareness, but not so long that you lose momentum and drive – it's like a full time job running a great campaign!

It's great to be ambitious, but also realistic. From our experience 87% of the campaigns that hit their goal will overfund by an average of 32%, therefore pick an attainable goal and hit it as soon as possible. The old adage no one likes to eat in an empty restaurant holds true with campaigns. People love getting involved with campaigns that have momentum and seem likely to succeed, and people don't stop funding. It also becomes an interesting PR story, e.g. "We blast through our goal in 24hrs' or X company doubled their funding goal in 5hrs!"

GET YOUR PITCH RIGHT

The first thing to do is to craft a clear and compelling message, then get in front of the camera and explain why you are so passionate about your business. Storytelling is key, explain what you are raising money for but also tell your story! A good two minute video explaining your project will help you raise 370% more money on average, and always remember that people fund people, not projects.

Secondly, consider your perks. Be as creative as possible and think about what will interest your potential audience. Start with between five and seven and you can add more throughout the campaign, as well as create impetus with featured perks, limited edition perks as it helps keep momentum after the initial wave of funding.

HAVE A TEAM TO SUPPORT YOU

Don't think of crowdfunding as a one man band. On average, campaigns with four or more people on the team will raise significantly more money than those who only have one person managing everything.

A campaign needs to be nurtured throughout - this is your child for the next 30-60 days! The more people you get to support you the better. Perhaps you know someone who is a social media whizz kid that can give you a hand, for example.

BE PRO ACTIVE

When you start a campaign it's crucial that you keep your funders, and potential funders engaged. Keep them updated on a regular basis, from our experience if you update the campaign at least three times raise you will raise on average 239% more than if you only update it two times, or less during their campaign.

Keeping up momentum is really important, if you get 25% of your funds during the first week you are five times more likely to hit your target or even surpass it. This is another reason having an attainable goal helps! We know that most of your funders will come from email campaigns, Facebook and Twitter, so don't forget to revamp your social media skills and start a conversation, you will definitely see the results coming through.

FIND YOUR AUDIENCE

The word 'crowdfunding' can be misleading, keep in mind that the initial people who fund your campaign will come from your network: your friends, family, colleagues. This is typically the first 30% and it's important to 'soft launch' to establish this base so that the wider Indiegogo community feels that they can trust the campaign and want to get involved. The next wave of funding will typically come from your close networks inner circle and the last funding is the 'stranger pounds'. This tends to be the largest cohort of people but it all depends on your early momentum.

It's so important to build your initial supporter base; you need to have an audience before the campaign starts. Think about your strategy and how you are going to attract and engage people outside your initial circle, either it's by going to networking events, exhibitions, partnering with organisations or associations, or by reaching out to press.

Having this in mind, remember to have your family and friends to help you get the ball rolling, no one will fund a campaign with zero contributions, so the more you can do initially the better. Then the trick is to be authentic, share your story and make it resonate with your audience.

AFTER THE CAMPAIGN

When the campaign is finished you need to fulfil your promise to those who have funded you. Whatever perks you offered, as rewards during your campaign need to be sent out to your community of funders. Make sure you deliver what you said you will and keep your funders updated on what's going on, they will appreciate it and hopefully become your early enthusiasts and evangelists – this can be invaluable for word of mouth marketing. You always want to delight and over-deliver rather than make your funders regret sharing in your vision.

There is a huge amount that goes into creating a successful campaign but we have created a plethora of educational resources to help wanting to run a campaign, we have mined 7 years of data and researched past campaigns to share our insights on what makes a great campaign.

NOTES

INTRODUCTION

[1] Snap (1990), *I've Got The Power*, Arista Records.

SECTION I

[2] Brian Rubinton, 2011, *Crowdfunding: Disintermediated Investment Banking*, FINE 547 Advanced Finance Seminar: McGill University.

[3] Chris Anderson, 2006, *The Rise of Crowdsourcing*, Wired.

[4] Giacomo Sardelli, 2012, *Further Up Yonder*, http://vimeo.com/54269169 [Accessed 02/07/2014]

[5] Fraser, S. & Lomax, S., 2011. *Access to Finance for Creative Industry Businesses*, London: Department for Business Innovation and Skills & Department for Culture, Media and Sport.

[6] The Mousetrap is the longest running theatre production in the UK. For more information see: http://en.wikipedia.org/wiki/The_Mousetrap

[7] Mark Rothko is an abstract expressionist artist.

[8] Rae, D., 2007. *Entrepreneurship: from opportunity to action*, Basingstoke;; New York: Palgrave Macmillan, p.3.

[9] Txt Stage was the first theatrical production produced by minivation in 2009. The troupe *Noise Next Door* performed ad lib comedy that incorporated text messages sent from the audiences' phones (which were projected live on stage). This performance formed part of a module for the award of MA in Cultural and Arts Management at University of Winchester.

[10] Financial Conduct Authority (*FCA*): http://www.fca.org.uk/
(See also this story from the BBC: http://www.bbc.co.uk/news/business-26439757)

[11] p2p Finance Association is the UK's trade body for interest (debt) model crowdfunding (crowdlending). For more information see: www.p2pfinanceassociation.org.uk

[12] UK Crowdfunding Association: a UK trade body covering all crowdfunding models. For more information see: www.ukcfa.org.uk

[13] EIS: http://www.hmrc.gov.uk/eis/index.htm

[14] SEIS: http://www.hmrc.gov.uk/seedeis/index.htm

[15] Deki: http://www.deki.org.uk/

[16] Kiva: http://www.kiva.org/

[17] Mythic: the story of Gods and men. By Little Monster Productions - campaign page on Kickstarter: https://www.kickstarter.com/projects/273246798/mythic-the-story-of-gods-and-men [Accessed 04/07/2014]

[18] Barnard, A. & Parker, C., 2012. *Campaign IT! : achieving success through communication*, London; Philadelphia: Kogan Page, p.9.

[19] For more on the geography of crowdfunding, see the original academic paper on this topic: Agrawal, A., K., Catalini, C. & Goldfarb, A., 2011. *The Geography of Crowdfunding*. Available at: http://www.nber.org/papers/w16820 [Accessed May 23, 2012].

[20] For a good view of why campaigns fail see: https://secure.huffingtonpost.com/lee-schneider/crowdfunding-fails_b_4171823.html

[21] Zhang, J. & Liu, P., 2012. Rational Herding in Microloan Markets. *Management Science*, 58(5), pp.892–912.

[22] Mitra, T. & Gilbert, E., 2014. The Language That Gets People to Give: Phrases That Predict Success on Kickstarter. In *Proceedings of the 17th ACM Conference on Computer Supported Cooperative Work #38; Social Computing*. CSCW '14. New York, NY, USA: ACM, pp. 49–61. Available at: http://doi.acm.org/10.1145/2531602.2531656 [Accessed July 4, 2014].

[23] Microco.sm campaign on Seedrs: https://www.seedrs.com/post_investment/8626 See also this Jeff Lynn interview: https://www.youtube.com/watch?v=U5NXu7hZzos

[24] For more on the link between Facebook likes and campaign success, see: Mollick, E.R., 2013. The Dynamics of Crowdfunding: An Exploratory Study, Rochester, NY: *Social Science Research Network*. Available at: http://papers.ssrn.com/abstract=2088298 [Accessed July 4, 2014].

[25] Rumelt, R., 2011. *Good Strategy Bad Strategy*, London, UK: Profile Books, p.11.

SECTION 2

[26] For more on 'Meet-up' see their pages at: http://www.meetup.com/ The extract from p.63 was taken from: http://www.meetup.com/Satellite-applications-catapult-Didcot/ [Accessed 02/10/13]

[27] Granovetter, M., 1973. The Strength of Weak Ties. *American Journal of Sociology*, 78(6), pp.1360–1380.

[28] Estimates vary wildly on how much initial funding should come from strong ties in order for a campaign to be successful. It does seem to be dependent on the model and the vision being crowdfunded.

[29] For the official 'Movember' UK site: http://uk.movember.com/

[30] For more on Social Capital see: https://en.wikipedia.org/wiki/Social_capital OR http://psychology.wikia.com/wiki/Social_capital

[31] For local advice on business related issues contact your local council. The economics officer may be the first point of contact to help you in this area.

[32] minivation started to compile their list (called simply 'listed') in 2013. It started out as a means of keeping track of the few innovative platforms that were in existence. However it has been updated at regular intervals and now boasts one the most comprehensive lists on the UK scene. Go to: http://minivation.org/listed.html

[33] People Per Hour: http://www.peopleperhour.com/
Others include:
99 Designs
Elance
Mechanical Turk
O'Desk
TaskRabbit

[34] Bentley, C., 2005. *I Want to Buy Your Product-- : have you sent me a letter yet?*, London: Sarceaux Publications.

years

building on our success

- 1993 Madrid
- 2007 Barcelona
- 2008 Mexico DF & Monterrey
- 2010 London
- 2011 New York & Buenos Aires
- 2012 Bogota
- 2014 Shanghai & San Francisco

BEYOND
THE WRITTEN WORD

Authors who speak to you face to face.

Discover LID Speakers, a service that enables businesses to have direct and interactive contact with the best ideas brought to their own sector by the most outstanding creators of business thinking.

- A network specialising in business speakers, making it easy to find the most suitable candidates.

- A website with full details and videos, so you know exactly who you're hiring.

- A forum packed with ideas and suggestions about the most interesting and cutting-edge issues.

- A place where you can make direct contact with the best in international speakers.

- The only speakers' bureau backed up by the expertise of an established business book publisher.

ABOUT THE AUTHOR

Chris Buckingham is a crowdfunding specialist. He has worked on campaigns ranging from the arts through to zoos and has contributed to over £2m worth of crowdfunding activity.

With a background in management of the creative and cultural industries he was one of the early users of crowdfunding.

His work with the crowdfunding community led to the establishment of the research and consultancy organisation minivation. Dedicated to raising awareness of the value of crowdfunding & gamification, minivation offers to help crowdfunding stakeholders achieve their goals.

He also lectures on the subject for both undergraduate and postgraduate courses at Winchester School of Art and University of Winchester. In addition to this Chris will be starting a fresh piece of research into crowdfunding and gamification in October 2015 at University of Southampton.

In this book, Chris covers for the first time all five models in the ecosystem.

CROWDFUNDING'S TIME HAS ARRIVED!

Through the power of the Internet raising monetary contributions from a large number of people is rapidly becoming a mainstream channel for raising funds.

Crowdfunding is not only a successful and exhilarating way to raise investment funds for projects but also enables exposure and can provide approval for ideas by the masses.

Crowdfunding is an extension of crowdsourcing, where people get together to generate ideas and solve problems, but here the crowd adds funds to a project. It offers investment solutions to all sorts of projects requiring funds, from apps to zoos.

Chris Buckingham, a crowdfunding specialist, provides a go-to bible for entrepreneurs and companies seeking investment. He provides unrivalled explanations and frameworks to help any entrepreneur or business to prepare and execute a successful crowdfunding campaign and raise the capital they need. It contains expert insights and advice from the major players in the sector, including the leading crowdfunding sites, on how success can be achieved.